THE MIDDLE WOODLAND POPULATION OF THE
LOWER ILLINOIS VALLEY: A Study
in Paleodemographic Methods

by
DAVID L. ASCH

Northwestern University
Archeological Program
SCIENTIFIC PAPERS, No. 1

Evanston, Illinois
1976

The Northwestern Archeological Program

Goals of the Program

The Northwestern University Archeological Program began in 1964 and has four objectives:

1. *To excavate and interpret the archeological record of the American Midwest.* It is believed that this record is at least 12,000 years long. All cultures in the Midwest prior to the 17th century were nonliterate. This means that written documentation is absent for more than 98 percent of the cultural history of the Great Lakes and prairie areas to the south. Archeological sites are the only remaining record of this prehistory.

   The Northwestern Archeological Program has focused its field activities on sections of the Illinois and Mississippi valleys where complex cultural developments occurred in prehistory. In many ways, it is believed, these valleys were the center of cultural development during most prehistoric periods. Yet these valleys are the scene today of urban and industrial expansion that has resulted in extensive destruction of archeological sites.

   It is imperative that research effort be focused on these valleys while they can still yield important archeological information.

2. *To develop and refine new archeological methods.* In the past 20 years American archeology has gone through more rapid change than perhaps in any comparable period before that time. Significant new goals—focusing on an understanding of cultural process—have been defined for archeology.

   Achieving these goals is dependent on new approaches to archeological research. These range from developing more effective institutional structures to support large-scale, programmatic research, to innovation in every phase of research performance from initial project design through excavation and laboratory analysis.

   The Northwestern Archeological Program is exploring a variety of field and laboratory methods that appear to have significant potential for increasing the archeologist's capacity for reading the prehistoric record. Through its Kampsville Archeological Center, it is attempting to develop more effective strategies for integrating 15 or more natural and social science disciplines in truly interdisciplinary research. These disciplines range from cultural anthropology to statistics, from nutrition to zoology.

3. *To provide a complete clinical training program geared to the needs of students becoming archeologists at a time when this science is undergoing rapid change.* Traditional graduate programs in universities generally have not incorporated many of the new techniques and methods of archeology into their curricula. The Northwestern Archeological Program is making these curriculum changes in an attempt to stimulate similar changes in other university archeological programs.

   A variety of clinical training courses have been developed in both archeology and collaborating disciplines. More than a dozen of these courses are now taught each year at the Kampsville Archeological Center during the Summer and Fall quarters.

4. *To develop an organized program for training scientists in the interfaces between archeology and various natural sciences (zoology, pollen analysis, geology, etc.).* These specialists, working with the archeologist, are able to develop models for environments on local and regional levels during thousands of years of

midwestern prehistory. Without them, the study of man-land relationships in prehistory is not possible. It is in this relationship that archeologists hope in part to discover general principles of cultural growth and decay.

Geographic Focus of the Field Program

The focus of the Northwestern Archeological Program is a 40- by 70-mile area immediately north of the confluence of the Illinois and Mississippi rivers. This area continued as a major center of prehistoric cultural development for thousands of years, a fact that probably relates to the incredibly rich and stable resources of the river floodplains.

Aside from its long and complex culture history, there are practical reasons why the lower Illinois Valley is an ideal field laboratory for the development of new methods and approaches in archeology: (1) Today this region is sparsely populated farmland, its southern limits separated from the St. Louis metropolitan area by the Mississippi River which has acted as an effective barrier to the northward spread of the city. Thus the lower Illinois Valley has escaped the widespread site destruction that has greatly reduced the archeological research potential of many comparable river valleys throughout the U.S. (2) The cost of performing research in the lower Illinois is as low as can be expected anywhere in the world. (3) Extensive information on climate, landforms, soils, water resources, flora and fauna is available on this region. These data provide an essential baseline for the cultural-ecological studies which are a major focus of NAP research.

The *cost* of doing archeological research has been too long overlooked as a significant factor affecting both the limitations archeologists impose on the goals of their research and the outcome of that research.

As long as archeological dollars are scarce, "cost" and "accessibility" are key factors when selecting an area for performing archeological fieldwork and experimenting with new methods. The cost of transportation between the University and the field, the cost of maintaining and operating a field headquarters, accessibility to cooperating natural scientists, accessibility to supplies and equipment, cost of transporting and maintaining students in the field, ability to maintain continuity in the field program in terms of political and economic factors, the prior availability of information on the natural environment (past and present), and the ease of transporting artifacts to the home institution and technical specialists to the field: All are factors which give the lower Illinois Valley a significant advantage as a testing ground for new archeological strategies and methods.

Educational Program

Research aside, the lower Illinois Valley provides an ideal environment for developing new educational programs in archeology. The 34 buildings of the Kampsville Archeological Center, 270 miles from the Evanston campus, present a retreat-like situation that enhances interaction between researchers and between researchers and students. Its dorm houses, dininghall, library, and other support facilities now enable the NAP to provide initial archeological field experience to an increasing number of students each year.

The Kampsville Center also provides an excellent context for the multidisciplinary training of professional archeologists. The summer and fall Kampsville programs combine training in excavation technique with laboratory experience in a number of disciplines relating specifically to archeology, e.g., botany, geology, and zoology. Resident instructors, each with his own teaching laboratory, train students in the rationale and techniques of their special disciplines. Some students excavate artifacts from a prehistoric village while others process the recovered materials through a diverse series of operations which range from the conventional analysis of artifacts to the study of plant and animal remains reflective of prehistoric subsistence and the study of snails and soils that disclose the environmental setting to which early cultures adapted.

Over several Summer or Fall quarters the student has the opportunity to participate in a variety of field and laboratory operations, thus providing him a sense of the various disciplines and how they integrate within the total research program.

Research Program

A major focus of the Northwestern Archeological Program has been the delineation of economic (particularly subsistence) activities, settlement patterns, and population changes that characterize the various phases of the Archaic, Woodland, and Mississippian periods ranging from 8000 B.C. to A.D. 1600. Efforts have been made to identify adaptive junctures, periods of significant change in the adaptations of lower Illinois Valley cultures. This work has led to the generation and testing of models that explain the observed shifts.

By 1975, more than 9 separate, but related research projects were underway in the lower Illinois Valley. Each of these, headed by one or more members of the NAP faculty, are conducted as separately defined projects, projects which have grown out of a series of closely reasoned questions stemming from earlier observations on the culture history of the lower Illinois region. Therefore in a very real sense the individual projects are mutually dependent and supportive; together they form a comprehensive approach to the culture history of a single world area.

The intensity of focus that the NAP has given lower Illinois Valley prehistory is unusual in archeology. There are both practical and philosophical reasons for the general lack of intensive research by archeologists into the prehistory of a single geographic area. Nonetheless, it is believed that such an intense focus, supported by an appropriate research design and a panoply of new methods and techniques, can produce a detailedness in the prehistoric data that will enhance observation of relationships between cultural variables, and between cultural variables and environmental and human biological variables, making possible the generation of significant explanatory models that might otherwise elude the archeologist. Only time will tell whether this geographically focused research effort will produce a significantly higher level of interpretation for archeology.

Publication of Research Results

Between 1969 and 1973, the Northwestern Archeological Program published eight research monographs in cooperation with the Illinois State Museum. These eight studies comprise the Research Papers series of the NAP; these volumes were also listed as numbers in the State Museum's *Reports of Investigations* series.

While this cooperation between institutions worked well, the growth of the archeological programs at both Northwestern University and the Illinois State Museum has made continuation of this publication arrangement impractical.

Therefore with the present volume by David Asch, the Northwestern Archeological Program begins the first publication of research under its own imprint. This series has the title *Scientific Papers.* It is hoped that the present volume, which explores population questions during the Middle Woodland period in the lower Illinois Valley, will begin the regular production of monographs and collective works that represent the research results of the Northwestern Archeological Program.

Stuart Struever
Evanston, Illinois

November, 1975

Contents

Figures

Tables

Preface

This manuscript is based upon a review of 100 years of archeological investigations in the lower Illinois Valley region. Its inception was in two papers that I wrote in 1970 for graduate courses at the University of Chicago and the University of Michigan. Subsequent versions were submitted as an MA research paper at the University of Chicago and as a doctoral candidacy qualifying paper at the University of Michigan.

The report is organized in the following manner: Chapter 1 introduces the problem and discusses potential uses for estimates of prehistoric population size and density.

In Chapter 2, the spatio-temporal limits for the study are defined, and methods of estimation are reviewed. Two methods depending on mortuary data are selected for estimating the regional population of the lower Illinois Valley 2,000 years ago.

Chapter 3 inquires into demographic assumptions underlying the population estimates and reconstructs the demographic structure of a Middle Woodland burial population. Information about demographic structure is used in testing the hypothesis that the burial population represents the deceased of a complete community, and it also supplies numerical values used in the population estimates that follow.

In Chapter 4, minimum and maximum estimates of regional population size and density are derived from the number of mound groups in the region and the size of their mortuary populations. A second maximum estimate of population levels is obtained by another method which utilizes mortuary data in conjunction with the number and size of habitation sites. Some directions for future refinements in the estimates are then enumerated.

The final chapter compares the prehistoric estimates from this study with data on historic Indian population levels, and it also contains a summary of the study.

I wish to express my appreciation to Dr. Jane E. Buikstra, Northwestern University, who made available to me extensive quantities of unpublished data on the burial populations of the Gibson and Klunk mounds. Many ideas presented in this paper are a product of discussions with her, and the citations do not adequately represent the extent of her contribution. She is not responsible, of course, for errors of interpretation or for the form in which the ideas and data are presented.

To Dr. Stuart Struever, Northwestern University, I am indebted for the intellectual and material contributions of the Northwestern University Archeological Program.

The financial support of a University of Chicago Graduate Fellowship and a National Science Foundation Graduate Fellowship during the preparation of this paper is gratefully acknowledged.

Special thanks are due to Mr. Robert Levis, Alton, Ill., for his longstanding interest in the Northwestern archaeological research program and specifically for his generosity in funding the publication of this study.

Information and criticism provided by the following persons are also deeply appreciated: Messrs. Kenneth B. Farnsworth and Michael D. Wiant and Miss Gail L. Houart, Northwestern University Archeological Program; Drs. James B. Griffin, Edwin N. Wilmsen, and Richard I. Ford, and Mr. Thomas K. Black, University of Michigan; and Mr. Thomas P. Volman, University of Chicago.

Special thanks are due to the editors of this manuscript: Joanne McKenzie, John McKenzie, and Barbara Collins.

David L. Asch
October, 1972

1

Introduction

Basically, the purpose of this study is to obtain estimates of regional population levels for the lower Illinois Valley during the Middle Woodland period. But because the results of prehistoric population estimates are frequently questionable and unreliable, I have dealt in depth with the data, methods, tests, and assumptions of population estimation—giving them an emphasis commensurate with the estimate itself.

The Middle Woodland period, dating between 150 B.C. and A.D. 400, is too remote to assume continuity between prehistoric and historic population levels. Little is known about prehistoric population sizes in eastern North America, and at least two major demographic shifts lie between the Middle Woodland and historic periods: (1) Near the end of the first millennium A.D., major population increases apparently accompanied the adoption of field agriculture. (2) Then, shortly after European contact, massive depopulation occurred as a result of the introduction of new diseases, competition for European trade, and differential access to European weapons. The difference in settlement frequency between Woodland and historic times is particularly striking in the lower Illinois Valley where more than 70 Middle Woodland habitation sites have been discovered, in contrast to archeological documentation for only two historic Indian sites.

In most regions and for most timespans, the information required for a population estimate is not readily available. Several factors commonly contribute to scanty and selective preservation of prehistoric skeletal populations, including destructive mortuary practices such as cremation, modern disturbance, and acid soils. Furthermore, archeological investigations have usually been insufficiently controlled or too sporadic to provide reliable information. However, in the lower Illinois Valley, Middle Woodland mortuary activities apparently resulted in little loss of skeletal materials. Subsequent destruction of the record of prehistoric populations by human activities and by natural processes is a greater problem, but less important than in many other regions. Past archeo-

logical work in the lower Illinois Valley provides a minimal basis for an estimate, and the long-term regional research commitment of the Northwestern University Archeological Program promises further refinements.

Although the estimates of this paper are for a single time and place, they provide a baseline for the demography of earlier times in eastern North America. The proto-agricultural hunter-gatherers of the Middle Woodland period found a most favored natural setting in the lower Illinois Valley, and the population density there was probably close to the maximum achieved in the eastern half of the continent before the development of major dependence on field agriculture.

1. THE QUESTION OF RELIABILITY

Two methods of estimating population size are employed in this study. Both require demographic information from completely excavated mortuary sites (mound groups). One method arrives at a regional estimate through information about the frequency of Middle Woodland mound groups; the other, less directly, from the frequency of village sites.

For any kind of numerical estimate obtained by sample or census, the question of reliability—and of measuring reliability—looms large. Glasgow's stern appraisal (1967) of Robert Ascher's prehistoric population estimate (1959) based on the subsistence remains of a California shell midden suggests that prehistoric population estimates are no different. Though Ascher's estimate was a plausible one, Glasgow showed that a large cumulative uncertainty resulted from lack of narrow limits for the values of variables entering into the estimate.

There are at least three dimensions to the analysis of reliability:

1. The adequacy of the archeological sample.
2. The completeness of the archeological record.

3. The realism of the theoretical assumptions.

The "sample" for the population estimate of this study is based upon a survey of published and unpublished archeological literature on the burial mounds and habitation sites in the research area. Because of the large scale data requirement for a regional estimate, an archeologist seldom is privileged to work with a data base accumulated specifically for estimating population size. Biases, then, are inevitable, and the apparatus of statistical theory is incapable of evaluating the most important sources of error. Still, it may be possible to specify maximum and minimum bounds for the values of variables entering into an estimate, permitting an assessment of reliability through the construction of maximum and minimum estimates of population size.

Questions of the completeness of the archeological record are more subtle since it is only possible to demonstrate that the record is incomplete, not to prove that it is adequately represented. However, there are reasonably powerful tests of completeness. Often it is possible to compensate for missing data indicated by these tests. Because population estimation involves assumptions that are not fully testable, independent lines for investigating population size should be developed. If the different lines converge, a stronger case can be built from their sum. Conversely, if the ranges for population size obtained by different methods do not intersect, the inadequacy of some of the assumptions is implied.

Since population levels of the past are not directly enumerable, there are also questions about theoretical assumptions underlying an estimate. These assumptions are predominantly demographic. It is not that the logic of the mathematical theory of demography is itself in question. Rather, the problem is that one must first be willing to make several simplifying assumptions in order to estimate population size from the size and age distribution of a prehistoric mortuary population. At best, real populations conform to these assumptions approximately. For archeologically documented populations, it is difficult to subject some of the assumptions to stringent tests. To this extent, untested propositions are introduced into the estimation procedure. Consequently, there is a need to examine what a statistician might term the "robustness" of the model; that is, to determine theoretically if population estimates are sensitive or insensitive to departures from the underlying assumptions.

The large portion of this paper devoted to specification of assumptions and assembly of evidence reflects an attempt to treat the questions of reliability explicitly. Certainly, there are areas for significant improvement at both the empirical and theoretical level, and in this sense the work is incomplete. However, my results are presented not merely as an exercise in method, but in the belief that additional investigation will refine rather than overthrow the estimates of this paper.

2. USES FOR AN ESTIMATE OF POPULATION DENSITY AND SIZE

As an isolated set of facts, prehistoric demography has little intrinsic value. However, the importance of demographic variables such as population size and density for the functioning and change of cultural systems is widely acknowledged. Bartholomew and Birdsell (1953:486), for example, assert that "one of the most critical ecological factors which can be determined about an animal is the density of its population." Hawley (1950:122) suggests that "size of population is doubtlessly one of the most important limiting factors in man's collective life," affecting both the extent of specialization and the complexity of social organization.

Putting the estimates obtained herein to use is not the aim of the present study. However, at this juncture I shall digress to consider the relevance of population size and density to anthropological studies. There are three main areas of discussion:

1. The manner in which environmental, demographic, and cultural variables interrelate in the ecosystem.
2. The potential uses of data on absolute population size and density in studies of population equilibrium and growth.
3. The merits of absolute versus relative measures of population in archeological studies.

Human Demography and Cultural Ecology

First, let us consider population data in the context of cultural ecology. Defining the discipline in the sense of Steward (1955) and Geertz (1963), cultural ecology examines selected cultural, demographic, biological, and geophysical processes within a region as a single system—the ecosystem. Variables are chosen from each of these spheres because of their pertinence to and regulative influence on the interchanges of matter and energy among the living and nonliving components of the system. Cultural components of the system include technological variables and any social relationships and ideas relevant to the distribution and regulation of matter and energy.

Cultural ecology raises functional questions regarding ecosystems—questions concerning their organization and regulation, their stability, and their interrelated changes (Geertz 1963). Thus, with a systems emphasis on mutual causal relationships, cultural ecology differs from environmental determinism, the search for direct causal effects of natural variables on the cultural realm. It also differs from environmental possibilism, which asserts that the environment has only passive significance for culture—setting broad limits within which a culture is free to choose from among many alternative methods for manipulating the environment. From the systems perspective of ecology, the components of an ecosystem "act collectively and simultaneously so that the action of any one factor is qualified by the others" (Cain 1944:17).

How do demographic variables articulate with other ecosystem components? Consider population density, a key variable closely connected with the rates at which matter and energy circulate through the system. Density is "a rough gauge of two aspects of settlement: (1) the physical spacing of individuals, or their accessibility to one another, and (2) the adaptation of population to land or, as this is sometimes phrased, population pressure" (Hawley 1950:100-101). Different densities pose different adaptive problems for a society; e.g., a lower value *potentially* increases isolation; a higher value potentially increases competition. But because the ecosystem contains adaptive components, these mechanical tendencies are not necessarily realized. Demographic determinism is as much an oversimplification of the relationship between demographic and cultural variables as environmental determinism is for environmental and cultural variables. However, neither is the relationship so arbitrary as to justify a retreat to demographic possibilism. When the predicted consequences of a density difference do not materialize, interesting questions arise about how and why some system components are protected from change.

Yengoyan's investigation (1968) of demographic and ecological influences on Aboriginal section systems throughout the Australian continent provides a good example of an adaptive response involving environmental, demographic,

and cultural variables. Among Australian tribes, kin relations are combined into zero, two, four, or eight categories (sections) which function in regulating marriage choices and in ritual and economic activities. Ideally, a tribesman's eligible marriage mates come from a single section. Yengoyan found that as the number of sections increases from two to four to eight, tribal area and population size also increase. He suggested that the ideal marriage rules cannot be sustained unless there are on the order of 25 eligible mates per section. Congruence between the ideal and empirical marriage systems thus implies larger minimum tribal populations when the number of sections is greater. Yengoyan also found that population density, which is highly and positively correlated with environmental favorability as measured by rainfall, correlates *inversely* with section number, tribal area, and tribal population. He interpreted the cooccurrence of large tribal populations and numerous marriage sections in regions where population is *more dispersed* as an adaptation to rigorous environmental circumstances. "One of the characteristics of section systems is the extension of section terms to distant kinsmen and nonkinsmen, who may occupy adjacent and distant areas of exploitation. The expansion of section terms not only combines spatially distant groups into meaningful units for marriage and ceremonial functions, but also permits reciprocal movements of related groups into larger territorial domains" (Yengoyan 1968:198-199). The potential for territorial expansion is important during times of unfavorable fluctuations in local resources. With more sections and greater tribal area, "right of entry" is gained for a larger region in the more arid parts of the continent. This adaptation tends to counter the inverse relation between isolation and population density predicted from the position of demographic determinism. Moreover, the relationship between environmental, demographic, and cultural variables is patterned to a degree unexpected from a possibilist's perspective.

Population Equilibrium and Growth

The dynamics of population growth and stability are central to ecology. Due to resource limitations, a high growth rate can be maintained for only a short time (on the archeologists' coarse time scale). Indeed, over the long run, the *average* annual per capita rate of growth approaches zero. The absolute growth during a long period may be large, but it will be far less than what is biologically feasible. Regulation, then, must be the rule for populations. An important set of population regulators are density-dependent; i.e., as a population grows, some factors act increasingly to lower fertility rates and/or to increase mortality rates until the net rate of change becomes negative. If a population declines, the reverse occurs: fertility rates rise and/or mortality rates decline.

Resource limitation is one major density-dependent variable. Initial assessments have been made of resource abundance for the Illinois Valley region (Zawacki and Hausfater 1969; Brown 1965; Munson, Parmalee, and Yarnell 1971; Parmalee, Paloumpis, and Wilson 1972), leading Struever (1968b) to conclude that this and similar riverine locations provided optimal environments in eastern North America for hunter-gatherers engaged in intensive collecting of harvestable foods. However, the population levels estimated in this paper seem low in comparison with estimates of the abundance of wild food in the region (Munson, Parmalee, and Yarnell 1971:413-415). Clearly, more work must be devoted to the elucidation of limiting factors such as scarcity during the poorest seasons and years and competition within and among groups.

Such research would be relevant to the more general problem of the extent to which the ratio of population to resources may vary (for a given technology). In many cases, the adjustment of population to resources seems poor. For example, in eastern North America, shortly after European contact, vast tracts of land were essentially uninhabited (Kroeber 1939). Indeed, many population geographers (e.g., Zelinsky 1966) see the lack of adjustment of modern population levels to resources more as the rule than the exception. Are recent times, marked by the worldwide European radiation and the advent of "death control," demographically exceptional in terms of this adjustment; or have such discrepancies been typical in most contexts? Do discrepancies become more pronounced at different geographic scales of investigation, and to what extent can they be attributed to the circumvention of local limiting factors by regional social organization? Is the equilibrium between density and resources very weak, such that populations are normally subject to wide fluctuations around a mean value? Some anthropological studies *have* found evidence for the close tracking of resources by population density (e.g., Birdsell 1953; Baumhoff 1963; Hainline 1965); but other cases have been advanced as evidence that productivity is normally well below the maximum achievable using the contemporary subsistence technology (Sahlins 1972). However, most studies of the population-resource relationship have been for societies that were partially integrated into the modern world economic system or that suffered severe depopulation as a result of Western contact. Population estimates for newly contacted nonliterate people by early explorers or colonists or derived from early documents very often are questionable (McArthur 1970). Consequently, the evaluation of theoretical predictions is difficult, and much of the burden of empirical demographic research necessarily falls upon the archeologist.

Birdsell (1968; see also 1953, 1957, and 1958) has suggested that, in addition to the density equilibrium system, there are other stable equilibrium systems operating in human populations and that predictable relationships exist between demographic variables and the balanced social, biological, and ecological forces contributing to the equilibrium. As an example of such a system, he states (1968:239) that "among generalized hunters, dependent upon local biota for their food sources, the local group averages 25 persons as a basement figure." If the group size falls below 25, social handicaps will develop, particularly involving marital exchanges of women. Larger groups, though not having the social handicaps, will exhaust resources of food and water, except in regions of abundance. Hence, local populations tend to be maintained at a steady level. Another equilibrium system, he suggests, maintains the size of dialectical tribes among hunter-gatherers at about 500 individuals; this equilibrium is largely independent of variations in the local biota, technology, or population density. In Australia, tribal boundaries are reported to inhibit intertribal social contacts (Birdsell 1958). Therefore, according to his argument, as the number of local groups in a dialectical tribe increases, the percentage of intertribal contacts declines because the tribal perimeter increases more slowly than the tribal area. This favors internal cultural and linguistic homogeneity, or heightens the contrast between tribes. At the same time, however, isolation by distance within the tribe is increased, which opposes tribal enlargement.

Population growth (or decline) exceeding normal fluctuations about a stationary mean is a sensitive indicator of fundamental cultural changes. Regardless of the reasons for population growth, growth itself has consequences for technology and social organization. Moreover, its accessibility to observation (including the prehistoric record) makes it an attractive variable for study.

One influential model for the relationship between population growth and subsistence evolution (Binford 1968) proceeds from the idea that population is normally in equilibrium at a level low enough not to tax the carrying capacity of the environment. If this equilibrium is disturbed, if the population outgrows the productive potential of the existing subsistence adaptation, strong incentive is engendered for development of subsistence techniques.

Another model is based on the idea of positive feedback. Minor initial deviations in a system are amplified by feedback until the system is radically changed. This is illustrated by developments in the system of wild grass procurement in Mesoamerica, which culminated after thousands of years in a major dependence on maize agriculture (Flannery 1968). Flannery postulated that after the initial genetic changes in wild maize made it more profitable to harvest, positive feedback operated in the following manner: "The more widespread maize cultivation, the more opportunities for favorable crosses and back-crosses; the more favorable genetic changes, the greater the yield; the greater the yield, the higher the population, and hence the more intensive cultivation" (1968:80).

Measures of sociocultural complexity and population size and density are positively, though roughly, correlated (Carneiro 1967; Sanders and Price 1968; Naroll 1956; Stevenson 1968; and Sahlins 1958). Although one can obtain no direct sociocultural conclusions from small differences of size or density, one perceives immediate implications from a fivefold or tenfold difference. For example, according to Sanders and Price (1968:85), a density of 1 person per square mile is typical of band or tribal levels of integration and perhaps of a few incipient chiefdoms; 10 per square mile, however, is beyond the range of bands and tribes and well within the range of chiefdoms. Because our knowledge of Middle Woodland sociocultural organization is still largely conjectural, the independent evidence of even a crude population estimate is useful.

Since demographic prerequisites may be expected for the development and persistence of many specialized social subsystems, it is reasonable to assume that population size should have *some*

relationship with the level of differentiation and organization of a society. Hawley (1950:122), for instance, remarks that "specialization presupposes a sufficient number of users of the given service to support a concentration of effort on its production," and it also requires a minimum level of social integration to regularize supply and demand.

Implications of demographic prerequisites for the nature of the Hopewell interaction sphere provide an illustration relevant to research in the lower Illinois Valley. Struever and Houart (1972) recently attempted to delineate interregional and interlocal distribution networks for Hopewell interaction sphere goods. They postulated that the flow of goods in and out of the lower Illinois Valley region was channeled through a single regional transaction center. Within the region, 6 to 12 evenly spaced sites served as second-level centers for the local distribution of exotic goods and the outward movement of local raw materials and products to the regional center, thence into the interregional transaction system. Struever and Houart were concerned primarily with establishing the formal spatial pattern of a three-level hierarchy of sites in the interaction sphere; they ventured few suggestions about the organization and maintenance of the system and the volume of materials passing through it.

Information about Middle Woodland population sizes should play a role in supplying these details. If my estimate of a maximum Middle Woodland density of 1 person per square mile (2,880 individuals) in the lower Illinois Valley region is correct, then for a population of this size the demand for exotic goods would have been small and could scarcely support specialists in long-distance trade. It would severely limit the development of a new, specialized organization for exchange and distribution apart from already existing social subsystems of more generalized function. A small volume of exchange provides little incentive for economic institutions to adjust supply and demand and to regularize exchange in time and space. In short, small populations provide little stimulus to growth of economic specialization in interregional transactions. The small population size suggests that the hierarchical spatial pattern described by Struever and Houart may reflect the loci for *use* for Hopewell interaction sphere goods more than the pattern of their distribution.

If extensive differentiation and complex organizations imply necessary minimum population levels, is the converse true? Do large size and high density beget diversified and highly complex societies? Though few see it as a sufficient cause, some social scientists believe population growth plays an important causal role in the evolution of social complexity. Among archeologists, William T. Sanders makes perhaps the most sweeping claims for the efficacy of numbers; for example, "the processes of societal evolution, . . . up to and including the level of the ancient state, were essentially demographic, particularly the increase of human beings per society" (Sanders and Marino 1970:101).

Durkheim's model (1933) for the influence of numbers on social complexity is reasonably representative of this viewpoint. He proposed (1933:262) that—

> The division of labor varies in direct ratio with the volume and density of societies, and, if it progresses in a continuous manner in the course of social development, it is because societies become regularly denser and more voluminous. . . .

We say, not that the growth and condensation of societies permit, but rather that they necessitate a greater division of labor. It is not an instrument by which the latter is realized; it is its determining cause.

By "density," Durkheim meant the "dynamic," "moral," or "social" density; that is, the frequency of intrasocietal relations. Social density is not only a function of the number of individuals per unit area, but also of the frequency of contacts and interchanges (communication and transportation) among the individuals. Durkheim qualified the effects of societal "volume" (i.e., size of population), stating that its influence is neither direct nor necessary. If a society grows by establishing more inclusive boundaries, greater division of labor is expected only if the number of social contacts increases thereby. Thus, a large "society" consisting of many isolated segments does little to elevate the division of labor above that fostered by the density of social relations within its segments.

Durkheim disagreed with the prevalent belief that man has an insatiable desire for "happiness" (e.g., for more leisure or greater material well-being) which leads man to seek greater efficiency and higher productivity, thereby supplying the impetus for development of the division of labor. (Sahlins [1972:2] gives a recent defense of the position that in most societies "material wants are finite and few, and the technical means unchanging but on the whole adequate.") Durkheim also

asserts that the increasing diversity of environments, exploited by geographically expanding societies, cannot provide this impetus. The driving force, Durkheim proposed, is the competition engendered by increasing volume and density. One adaptation to increasing competition is occupational specialization. By decreasing the number of individuals who must seek the same material and social resources to make their living, it ameliorates the intensity of demand for limited resources.

Durkheim's model allows the possibility that expected social effects of a change in population density may be nullified by changes in mobility (communication and transportation). Thus, social variables enter into the determination of the extent of the division of labor. Sanders and Marino (1970:101) suggest, however, that the potential for changes in communications technology prior to the Industrial Revolution was slight and, hence, that population growth was generally the overriding factor in preindustrial social evolution. Perhaps in a broad sense the latter statement can be defended, but Service (1962:72), while acknowledging a close correspondence between evolutionary levels and the size and density of the social body, can nonetheless observe "a lack of congruity between ecology and demography on the one hand, and social structure, or its relative absence, on the other" in band level societies. The section system in Australia, cited previously, provides another example of density differences counteracted by changes in mobility and communication.

Absolute Versus Relative Measures of Size

Regional population size and density are but two of many important absolute population statistics. Others, enumerated by Struever (1971), are size and variation in coresidential units at the household and settlement level; size of the maximum local aggregate and the minimum subsistence-settlement unit; and the size of the minimal, intermediate, and maximal sociopolitical units. Presently in the lower Illinois Valley, regional size and density are, I believe, the only absolute measures of population for which the methodological assumptions are sufficiently convincing and the prehistoric data base sufficiently reliable to justify an estimate.

Measures of relative size or of changes in population, however, can often be obtained more easily than absolute size because variables linked to population size, e.g., settlement area and debris frequency, can be observed even when the relationship cannot be calibrated in absolute terms. Information on the relative size of populations is useful in the investigation of population regulation (Zubrow 1971). Population pressure, a critical factor in many adaptive changes (Binford 1968; Harner 1970), can be detected by changes in relative size. In general, population change is often an indicator of deep-seated transformations in a cultural system, whether the former occur as a cause or consequence of the latter (Sanders and Price 1968). For the lower Illinois Valley, Struever (1968a,b) began the study of relative size as part of an investigation of adaptive changes and correlated population growth between the Early and Middle Woodland periods. The need and potential for continued investigations of relative size in the region is great.

While measures of relative size are indispensible to prehistoric studies, the preceding discussion has suggested a number of problems for which only absolute measures will suffice. The latter are particularly valuable when dealing concretely with the limiting factors of a regulated system and, also, when demographic prerequisites for the development of specialization and complex organization are evaluated. Finally, for many population comparisons, a common measure of relative size will be lacking (e.g., for a prehistoric society and an ethnographically documented one) so that the comparison must be based on absolute size.

2

The Setting and Methods

Chapter 2 is concerned first of all with carefully ascertaining the length of the Middle Woodland period and defining the geographic extent of the region, since the space-time limits of the study appear as numerical factors in the estimation formulas.

Next, I describe various methods of estimating population levels and, simultaneous to the discussion, present arguments for and against their use.

1. SPATIO-TEMPORAL LIMITS

Determining the Length of the Middle Woodland Period

The Middle Woodland period is the smallest temporal unit that could be adequately defined and dated for the purposes of this study. According to Struever's syntheses (1960, 1968b), Middle Woodland in the lower Illinois Valley is coextensive with the Havana-Hopewell and Pike-Hopewell cultural phases. Havana and Hopewell series pottery are diagnostic of the former phase and Pike and Baehr pottery of the latter (Struever 1968b:140-173; Griffin 1970:8). Some projectile point styles probably associate differentially with these pottery styles (Montet-White 1968), but a one-to-one correspondence has not been demonstrated. Struever (1960) also suggests that the pottery styles are found at different intervals along an inferred temporal sequence of changing mortuary practices. No other distinctive features have been proposed for the two phases.

While Havana and Hopewell pottery styles undoubtedly appear prior to Pike and Baehr (Struever 1960, 1968b; Griffin 1952, 1970; Powell 1957), their mutually exclusive occurrence in a stratigraphic sequence has never been observed. Nor does radiocarbon dating substantiate temporally disjunct styles (Table 1). Settlement patterns associated with the proposed phases appear to be identical and a high proportion of all Middle Woodland sites in the region yield both Havana-Hopewell and Pike-Baehr pottery (Struever 1968b:195-218; 1968c:303-308). Thus, consider-

able temporal overlap of Havana-Hopewell and Pike-Baehr pottery remains a possibility. If such overlap occurs, it is far from evident that the pottery styles are associated with distinctive social units. For these reasons the population estimate must be extended over the entire Middle Woodland period.

In this paper estimates of man-years lived during the Middle Woodland period are divided by its length to arrive at an estimate of the average regional population level. Hence, it is necessary to evaluate radiocarbon evidence for the boundaries between Early, Middle, and Late Woodland periods.

Of the 35 Middle Woodland C^{14} dates from sites in the lower Illinois and adjacent Mississippi Valleys, 28 cluster between the 320-year timespan of 70 B.C. and A.D. 250 (Table 1). There are 4 prior to 70 B.C. The date of 550 B.C. ±150 from the Pool site is based on mussel shell and is clearly unreliable. The other 3 early outliers lie within 2 standard deviations of 70 B.C. and could possibly have resulted from counting errors. The 2σ upper bound for the Macoupin site date of 460 B.C. is 40 B.C. Notwithstanding the statement appearing in the University of Michigan radiocarbon laboratory report (Crane and Griffin 1966:265), Sample M-1403 from the Peisker site does not occur in a clear Middle Woodland context. Struever (1968b:157-158) remarks that the sample was excavated "from a mixed Black Sands-Initial Havana midden underlying Peisker Mound 1" and that it "may be associated with the Black Sand [Early Woodland] phase." Accompanying the report of the 160 B.C. ±130 radiocarbon date from Montezuma Mound 9 was the following comment by the excavator, Gregory Perino: "Date seems early for this mound group, but sample may be from inner section of log" (Crane and Griffin 1968:69). Even the date of 70 B.C. ±200 from the Macoupin site is suspect because of technical problems encountered in running the sample (Crane and Griffin 1972b).

Besides the questionable Black Sand-Initial Havana date mentioned above, there are only four

Early Woodland dates from the lower Illinois Valley, all from the Peisker site. Two of these possibly date the latest Early Woodland phase (Black Sand, as represented by Liverpool ceramics).

The transition from the Black Sand to Havana phase in the lower Illinois Valley almost certainly occurs prior to 70 B.C., the beginning of the swarm of Middle Woodland dates. Since Sample M-1403 from Peisker must be either the latest Early Woodland date or the earliest acceptable Middle Woodland date from the region, 230 B.C. seems the earliest reasonable date for dividing Early from Middle Woodland.

To take up the question of a terminus for the Middle Woodland period, there are only 3 Middle Woodland dates later than A.D. 250. These and the 2 earliest *acceptable* dates for early Late Woodland phases in the region (White Hall and Weaver) all fall within the fifth century A.D. A 100-year hiatus follows, and then 9 more White Hall and Weaver dates are reported for A.D. 600 and later. Thus, the 350-year period between A.D. 250 and A.D. 600 is inadequately represented by five overlapping Middle and early Late Woodland dates. Certainly, the end of the Middle Woodland period should be placed after A.D. 250. But it probably occurs by A.D. 460, the latest C^{14} date from a Middle Woodland context.

This radiocarbon chronology suggests a minimum span of Middle Woodland occupation of 320 years (70 B.C. to A.D. 320) and a maximum timespan of 690 years (230 B.C. to A.D. 460). In this study we shall employ a compromise between these extremes. Taking into consideration the range of lower Illinois Valley dates as well as subsidiary information from other regions, Struever (1968b) prefers a Middle Woodland period of 550 years—between 150 B.C. and A.D. 400. This is reasonably close to a median between the extremes, and it is the timespan I have chosen for the population estimates.

The uncertainty in the length of the Middle Woodland period is a major flaw in the estimates. However, it is one factor for which the reliability will surely improve in the normal course of archeological research.

Definition of the Research Region

The population estimates pertain to a region essentially equivalent to Struever's defined research universe (1968b:85). This region comprises the drainage basin of the lower section of the Illinois River, including all the tributary streams entering the Illinois Valley between the mouth of the river and the Morgan-Cass County line 67 miles to the north (Fig. 1). Points 50 miles from the main valley fall within this region. The area of the lower Illinois drainage basin is 2,880 square miles.

Population densities are also calculated for a second, smaller region—a 15-mile-wide transect of the lower Illinois Valley that includes the 4-to-5-mile-wide valley and the 5 or 6 miles of wooded upland on either side. Its area is 1,000 square miles.

The definition of spatial boundaries has important implications for interpreting population densities. Because Middle Woodland sites are concentrated in major river valleys, boundaries delimiting zones of intensive exploitation will produce densities quite different from those delimiting a maximal territory of exploitation.

Ethnohistorical inquiries into population densities of eastern North America have used the maximal region as the basic unit. However, densities for regions of intensive exploitation may have greater social and ecological significance. Meaningful comparisons of lower Illinois Valley population densities with those of other areas and times will thus require a reevaluation of the concept of population density itself. A density estimate comparable to those usually made for the historic Eastern Woodlands would necessitate an extension of the research universe even farther to the east, at least halfway to the Kaskaskia or Wabash rivers.

It should also be noted that the area of investigation is adjacent to a region of the Mississippi Valley that probably supported a population equal in size to that of the Illinois Valley. Maximal prehistoric sociopolitical units are likely to have embraced both valleys. Consequently, if the population estimates in this paper seem small for the complex political systems sometimes suggested for the Middle Woodland period, they may be more acceptable if account is taken of a substantial Mississippi Valley contribution to population size. Though it is preferable to work within a region having limits defined by boundaries of prehistoric social or cultural units, this is presently impossible due to the relative lack of archeological investigations, particularly of mound surveys, in the adjacent Mississippi Valley and also because of the difficulty of delimiting such prehistoric units.

TABLE 1. Woodland Radiocarbon Dates for the Lower Illinois Valley

Period and site	Lab no.	Date[a]	Cultural association	Sources
Early Woodland:				
Peisker, Submound 2, Level C	0-2266	625 B.C. ±110	Peisker (?)[b]	Struever 1968b
Peisker, Submound 2, Level C	—	480 B.C. ±130	Peisker (?)	Struever 1968b
Peisker, Submound 2, Levels A-C	M-1404	325 B.C. ±135	Peisker or Black Sand	Crane and Griffin 1966
Peisker, Submound 2, Level C	0-2270	250 B.C. ±110	Peisker (?)	Struever 1968b
Middle Woodland:				
Pool	M-15[c]	550 B.C. ±150	Havana- or Pike-Hopewell	Crane 1956
Macoupin	M-2226	460 B.C. ±210	Havana-Hopewell	Crane and Griffin 1972b
Peisker, Submound 1	M-1403	230 B.C. ±130	Black Sand or Initial Havana	Crane and Griffin 1966
Montezuma, Mound 9	M-1485	160 B.C. ±130	Havana- or Pike-Hopewell	Crane and Griffin 1968
Macoupin	M-2225	70 B.C. ±200	Havana-Hopewell	Crane and Griffin 1972b
Loy	ISGS-181	60 B.C. ± 85	Havana-Hopewell	Farnsworth pers. comm.
Peisker, Submound 2, Level A[d]	—	40 B.C. ±160	Havana-Hopewell (?)	Struever 1968b
Kamp, Submound 9	M-1040	30 B.C. ± 75	Pike-Hopewell (?)	Crane and Griffin 1962
Loy	ISGS-171	20 B.C. ± 75	Havana-Hopewell	Farnsworth pers. comm.
Loy	ISGS-251	20 B.C. ± 75	Havana/Pike-Hopewell	Farnsworth pers. comm.
Macoupin	M-2229	0 ±200	Havana-Hopewell	Crane and Griffin 1972b
Bedford, Mounds 10-11	M-444	A.D. 10±125	Havana- or Pike-Hopewell	Crane and Griffin 1958b
Kamp, Mound 9	M-1039	A.D. 10± 75	Pike-Hopewell	Crane and Griffin 1962
Bedford, Mounds 10-11	M-443	A.D. 20±125	Havana- or Pike-Hopewell	Crane and Griffin 1958b
Macoupin	M-2243	A.D. 50±140	Havana-Hopewell	Crane and Griffin 1972b
Snyders	M-1154	A.D. 60± 75	Havana-Hopewell	Crane and Griffin 1963
Peisker, Submound 3	M-1570	A.D. 70±120	Havana-Hopewell[e]	Crane and Griffin 1968
Peisker, Submound 3	M-2223	A.D. 90±140	Havana-Hopewell	Crane and Griffin 1972b
Peisker, Submound 2, Level A[d]	0-2269	A.D. 100±105	Havana-Hopewell (?)	Struever 1968b
Snyders	M-1487	A.D. 100±120	Havana- or Pike-Hopewell	Crane and Griffin 1965
Peisker, Submound 2, Level A[d]	—	A.D. 130±160	Havana-Hopewell	Struever 1968b
Kamp, Mound 9	M-1041	A.D. 140± 75	Pike-Hopewell	Crane and Griffin 1962
Klunk, Mound 1	M-1161	A.D. 175± 75	Havana-Hopewell	Crane and Griffin 1963
Peisker, Submound 2, Level A[d]	M-1405	A.D. 180±130	Havana-Hopewell (?)	Crane and Griffin 1966
Kamp, Mound 9	M-1038	A.D. 190±100	Havana-Hopewell	Crane and Griffin 1962
Pool	M-183	A.D. 210±125	Pike-Hopewell	Crane 1956
Macoupin	M-2245	A.D. 220±130	Havana-Hopewell	Crane and Griffin 1972b
Schafner, Mound 1	M-2187	A.D. 220±140	Havana-Hopewell	Crane and Griffin 1972b
Snyders	M-1155	A.D. 230± 75	Havana-Hopewell	Crane and Griffin 1963
Bedford, Mound 4	M-445	A.D. 230±125	Havana- or Pike-Hopewell	Crane and Griffin 1958b
Peisker, Submound 3	M-1569	A.D. 250±120	Havana-Hopewell	Crane and Griffin 1968
Knight, Mound 8	M-164[c]	A.D. 250±150	Pike-Hopewell	Crane 1956
Bedford, Mound 9	M-446	A.D. 400±125	Havana- or Pike-Hopewell	Crane and Griffin 1959
Macoupin	M-2245	A.D. 450±130	Havana-Hopewell	Crane and Griffin 1972b
Apple Creek[f]	OWU-105B	A.D. 460±175	Havana-Hopewell	Ogden and Hay 1967
	M-1721	A.D. 460±130	Pike-Hopewell	Crane and Griffin 1968

TABLE 1 (Cont.).

Late Woodland:

Period and site	Lab no.	Date[a]	Cultural association	Sources
Apple Creek	M-1408	710 B.C. ±130	White Hall	Crane and Griffin 1966
Koster, East Field	GX-2400	A.D. 325±100	Early Bluff	Struever pers. comm.
Stilwell	M-1263	A.D. 400±120	White Hall	Crane and Griffin 1964
Bridgewater	M-1998	A.D. 480±130	White Hall	Crane and Griffin 1970
Perrins Ledge Crematory	M-2254	A.D. 570±150	"Bluff"	Crane and Griffin 1972a
Klunk, Mound 8	M-1355	A.D. 600±110	Early Bluff[g]	Crane and Griffin 1964
Stilwell	M-1262	A.D. 620±120	White Hall	Crane and Griffin 1964
Newbridge	M-2002	A.D. 620±400	White Hall	Crane and Griffin 1970
Apple Creek	M-1406	A.D. 640±110	White Hall	Crane and Griffin 1966
Snyders	M-714	A.D. 640± 75	Early Bluff[g]	Crane and Griffin 1962
Koster, East Field	GX-2399	A.D. 640±100	Early Bluff	Struever pers. comm.
Koster, Mound 2	M-1357	A.D. 650±120	Early or Late Bluff	Crane and Griffin 1966
Newbridge	M-2000	A.D. 660±130	White Hall	Crane and Griffin 1970
Apple Creek	M-2001	A.D. 700±130	White Hall	Crane and Griffin 1970
Irving	M-489	A.D. 770±125	Weaver	Crane and Griffin 1958a
Klunk, Mound 10	M-1356	A.D. 780±120	Early Bluff[g]	Crane and Griffin 1966
Apple Creek	M-1407	A.D. 790±120	White Hall	Crane and Griffin 1966
Bridgewater	M-1999	A.D. 900±200	White Hall	Crane and Griffin 1970
Apple Creek	M-1997	A.D. 920±120	White Hall	Crane and Griffin 1970
Perrins Ledge Crematory	M-2253	A.D. 1000±150	"Bluff"	Crane and Griffin 1972a

[a]Dates given in terms of Libby half-life of 5,570 years; 1 standard deviation error limits are quoted, except for University of Michigan dates published prior to 1963, for which error limits are a *minimum* of 1 standard deviation (Crane and Griffin 1963:228).

[b]Struever (1968b) divides Black Sand phase into an earlier Peisker subphase and a later Black Sand subphase.

[c]Date is on shell.

[d]Sample may be intrusive into Level A.

[e]See Struever (1968b:142,159,165) for assessment of cultural affiliation.

[f]Same sample.

[g]Assessment of Early Bluff cultural association follows Munson (1971:14).

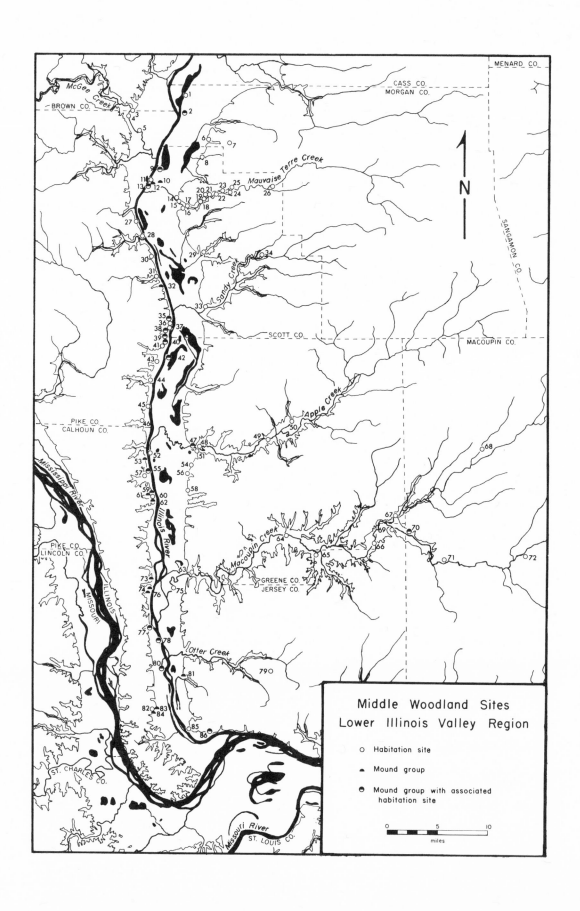

Middle Woodland Sites
Lower Illinois Valley Region

○ Habitation site

▲ Mound group

◑ Mound group with associated habitation site

0   5   10
miles

The Gibson-Klunk Mounds and
Their Associated Habitation Site

Demographic information from the mortuary populations of the Gibson and Pete Klunk mound groups figures prominently in the population estimates. These groups and the superficially investigated Ben Klunk group are located on bluff crests at the western margin of the lower Illinois Valley, in Calhoun County, at a point where Kampsville Creek, a small secondary stream enters the main valley. The mound groups overlook The Gardens of Kampsville, a large Middle Woodland habitation site extending along the talus slope of the bluffs. The general location of these archeological sites is indicated in Figure 1, a regional map of Middle Woodland mound groups and habitation sites.

The Gibson mound group lies on the blufftop south of the east-west-oriented Kampsville Hollow, and the Ben Klunk and Pete Klunk mound groups are located on the bluff north of the hollow. The latter two groups lie on ridge crests at either side of a tertiary creek that flows into Kampsville Creek. There is also a single unnamed mound lying on the ridge between Kampsville Creek and the Ben Klunk group. Figure 2 shows the location of these sites at the mouth of Kampsville Hollow.

Figure 1. Distribution of Middle Woodland sites in the lower Illinois Valley. Map is assembled from information in survey files of the Northwestern University Archeological Program.

1 Sunset Beach
2 Meredosia-Hilderbrand mound group and Meredosia habitation site
3 Pool
4 Irving
5 Hinners
6 Rausch-Lansink
7 Spring Run
8 Marsh
9 Naples Abbott mound group and habitation site
10 Naples Chambers mound group
11 Emeline
12 Robertson mound group
13 Naples Castle mound group and habitation site
14 Bridge
15 Oxville
16 Thomas
17 Mauvaise Terre-Merriman
18 Matthews
19 Calving
20 Hubbard
21 Exeter
22 Meier
23 Magelitz
24 Krems
25 Merritt
26 Grundy
27 Ceisler
28 Blue Creek
29 Plum Creek
30 Manker-Little League-Monta
31 Swartz-Florence
32 Swartz mound group
33 Sand Creek Church
34 Andell-Watt
35 Montezuma mound group and Bixby habitation site
36 Wheeler
37 Ina Knox
38 Bedford mound group and Bedford-Pearce habitation site
39 Pilot's Peak mound group and Lyons habitation site
40 Helm mound group and Buckhorn habitation site
41 Springer
42 Mound House mound group and habitation site

43 Gourley
44 Pulpwood Mill
45 Hatcher
46 Vaughn
47 Apple Creek mound group and habitation site
48 Audrey
49 McPherson
50 Crooked Run
51 Camerer
52 Newport Landing
53 Brangenberg mound group
54 Hobson
55 Kamp mound group and habitation site
56 Bluffdale-Russell
57 Rapp
58 Levis
59 Pete Klunk mound group
60 The Gardens of Kampsville
61 Ben Klunk mound group
62 Gibson mound group
63 Titus-Upper Macoupin
64 Crane
65 Devor
66 Loy
67 Edwards
68 Hettick
69 Flautt
70 Gracey mound group and Chism habitation site
71 Orange
72 Spanish Needle
73 Hagen mound group
74 L'Orient mound group
75 Macoupin
76 Hardin mound group
77 Merrigan mound group and habitation site
78 Peisker mound group and habitation site
79 Erickson
80 Tom Collins mound group and habitation site
81 Parsell mound group
82 Kiel
83 Meppen mound group
84 Hazelherst mound group
85 Marquette
86 Duncan Farm mound group and habitation site

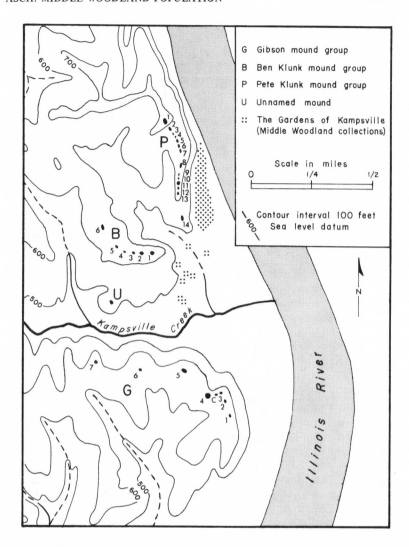

Figure 2. Location of archeological sites at the mouth of Kampsville Hollow. Map is based on information provided by Gregory Perino and Kermit Suhling (personal communication), from the survey files of Northwestern University Archeological Program, and from maps in Perino (1973a:59) and Buikstra (1972).

The proximity of all three mound groups to The Gardens of Kampsville suggests that their burials should be treated as a single mortuary population. Jane Buikstra (1972) states that the populations of the Gibson and Pete Klunk groups are biologically indistinguishable but are significantly different from both the Peisker-Collins and Bedford series excavated from other Middle Woodland mound groups of the lower Illinois Valley. Buikstra also notes that burial programs in the Gibson and Pete Klunk mounds are identical. For these reasons, it is plausible that the burials of the Gibson-Klunk mounds constitute The Gardens of Kampsville mortuary population.

Seven mounds constitute the Gibson group, and the Ben Klunk and Pete Klunk groups number 6 and 14, respectively. Archaic, Middle Woodland,

and Late Woodland burials were found in the Gibson and Pete Klunk groups. Also, Mississippi burials were found in Mound 14 of the Pete Klunk group. Nevertheless, the cultural affiliation of most skeletal material was determined. Gregory Perino directed the complete excavation of the Pete Klunk mounds (and intermingled natural knolls) in 1960-1961 and, with Jane Buikstra, supervised the Gibson excavations in 1969. The excavations yielded remains of 372 Middle Woodland individuals from the Pete Klunk group and 161 from Gibson. Field reports of the Klunk investigations are available (Perino 1968, 1973a), and Perino is presently preparing a report on the Gibson mounds. Brief reports of the Klunk Middle Woodland burials have been published by King B. Hunter (1965) and Robert Blakely (1971). Jane

Buikstra's doctoral thesis (1972) is a study of the biology of the skeletal series from the Gibson and Pete Klunk mounds and an analysis of mortuary practices. (It will appear as Volume 2 of this publication series.) I have drawn upon her evaluations of age and sex for the burials of both mound groups.

The mound groups had been opened prior to the work of Perino and Buikstra in the 1960's. As early as 1888, James Middleton conducted limited excavations in the Pete Klunk and Ben Klunk mound groups (Middleton 1888; Thomas 1894:126-129), and there is also a brief record of the depredations of relic collector L. E. Gibson into the mound group bearing his name (Perino 1968:119-123; Titterington n.d.[a]:73). Though the mounds bore the scars of numerous other unrecorded probes, Perino and Buikstra were able to recover all but a small proportion of the Middle Woodland burial population from the Gibson and Pete Klunk groups. Further discussion of mound disturbance is presented in Chapter 4, Section 1.

The Gardens of Kampsville habitation area lies within the present town of Kampsville. Formerly, two named areas of Middle Woodland debris scatter were recognized within Kampsville—the Terneus and Klunk Hill-Bottom sites (Struever 1968b:314-315, 394). Ground cover and slope-wash obscured the limits of these sites, and Struever recognized that they might be two parts of a single large habitation area. "Huge quantities of Hopewell debris" were exposed between the foot of the bluff below the Pete Klunk mounds and Illinois Route 100 when fill was removed for construction of the highway in the 1920's (Perino 1968:12). Recently, collections of debris have been obtained from several gardens, stream cuts, and outhouse excavations in Kampsville, and undoubtedly a continuous linear scatter exists, extending for at least ½ mile. Struever has re-named the total scatter as The Gardens of Kampsville. If the width of the scatter is an average of only 100 feet—and it is probably much greater—the total site area would be 6 acres, making this one of the larger Middle Woodland habitation areas of the lower Illinois Valley.

2. METHODS

Numerous methods have been proposed to estimate population size. They fall into three generic categories:

1. *Habitation area.* Correlations of a measure of habitation area (or a count of structures) with population size, where the two variables are calibrated from an examination of the relationship in historically documented societies.
2. *Environmental carrying capacity.* Arguments based on the carrying capacity of the natural environment.
3. *Man-years.* Measurements of the cumulative number of years lived by a population over a known timespan, either directly from a burial population or indirectly through artifacts and habitation debris whose frequencies are dependent on man-years of occupation.

Habitation Area

In the first category of estimates, the simplest procedure for estimating the population of a community is to multiply the number of house structures by the presumptive mean household size, the latter factor being obtained by ethnographic analogy. This approach is exemplified by the work of Ricketson (1937) and Haviland (1965, 1969, 1972) for the Maya and of Cook and Heizer (1965, 1968) for California Indians. However, several problems attend this approach. As Sanders and Price (1968:164-165) and Thompson (1971) note, structures at a site may not be contemporaneous or at least not contemporaneously occupied even if all are standing at one time, and in eastern North America style chronologies are too crude to permit relative dating of houses to within a few years. Second, extensive excavations at a number of Middle Woodland habitation sites in the lower Illinois Valley have disclosed very few house patterns. Possibly the flimsiness of most structures, and the destruction and masking of post-mold patterns during long prehistoric occupations of a site are largely responsible for the failure to delineate them. There is no assurance, then, that even a long-term program of research in the region will reveal sites where all house patterns are preserved. A third problem is choosing a value for household size. The direct historical approach was used by Ricketson and Haviland and by Cook and Heizer, but it is inappropriate for a Middle Woodland estimate.

An alternative method is to estimate the population of a community from measurements of the total floor area by calibrating the two variables on the basis of ethnographic investigations of their relationship. If successful, this method eliminates the problem of estimating household size. However, the difficulties of finding house structures and of demonstrating their contemporaneity are attendent with this method as well.

Naroll's correlation (1962) of total area of dwelling floors and settlement population is widely used by archeologists. Drawing on a global sample of historically documented societies, he proposed the following relationship (1962:587):

> Total area of the dwelling floors and total population of the largest settlements of 18 societies show a loglog regression which suggests that the population of a prehistoric settlement can be very roughly estimated as of the order of one-tenth the floor area in square meters.

As Naroll himself admits, floor area is indeed a *very rough* predictor of population size. This is evident from Table 2 in which observed settlement population is expressed as a percentage of the predicted size for the same 18 societies from which Naroll's relationship was generated and for 4 others included in LeBlanc's discussion (1971).

The relationship of

$$\text{Population} = 1/10 \text{ (floor area)}$$

is an approximation to Naroll's loglog regression equation of floor area on population. To provide the most favorable correspondence between expected and predicted values, the predicted values in Table 2 are calculated from the loglog regression obtained when population is treated as the dependent variable:

$$\text{Predicted population} = 0.28589 \text{ (floor area)}^{0.91466} \qquad (2\text{-}1)$$

Of the 18 societies sampled by Naroll, 8, or 44 percent, were either less than one-half or more than twice the predicted value; 2, or 11 percent, were either less than one-third or more than 3 times the predicted value. Two of the observed population values for the four societies of LeBlanc's addendum were less than one-half the value predicted from Naroll's study.

TABLE 2. *Ratios of Observed Settlement Population to Population Size Predicted by Naroll's Formula, in a Worldwide Sample of Societies*[a]

| Sample society | Observed population | Data for 2 prediction methods | | | |
| | | Loglog regression equation | | 1/10 (floor area)[b] | |
		Predicted population	Ratio of observed to predicted	Predicted population	Ratio of observed to predicted
Bella Coola	400	2,039	0.20	1,632	0.25
Iran (Hasanabad)	182	540.5	.34	382.2	.48
Ramkokamekra	298	825.8	.36	607.5	.49
Tonga	5,000	11,820	.42	11,150	.45
Kazak	3,000	7,014	.43	6,300	.48
Wachipaeri	29	59.27	.49	34.1	.85
Hupa	200	365.2	.55	249.0	.80
Klallam	200	355.8	.56	242.0	.83
Ila	3,000	5,365	.56	4,700	.64
Ifaluk	252	436.3	.58	302.4	.83
Barama River Caribs	47	65.69	.72	38.1	1.23
Samoa	1,132	1,506	.75	1,172	.97
Eyak	120	134.6	.89	83.6	1.35
Vanua Levu	75	70.59	1.06	41.3	1.82
Tikopia	1,260	1,131	1.11	857.0	1.47
Wintun	200	144.0	1.39	90.0	2.22
Iroquois	3,000	1,699	1.77	1,337	2.24
Kiwai	400	220.7	1.81	143.2	2.79
Zulu	15,000	7,281	2.06	6,561	2.29
Cuna	1,800	749.0	2.40	546.0	3.30
Kapauku	181	62.59	2.89	36.2	5.00
Inca	200,000	17,130	11.67	16,720	11.96

[a]Based on Naroll's (1962) sample, except for the following societies discussed by LeBlanc (1971): Samoa, Iran (Hasanabad), Wachipaeri, and Barama River Caribs.
[b]Floor area measured in square meters.

Another complicating factor is that the relationship of population to floor area is likely to vary systematically from region to region, so that in some areas Naroll's formula will give consistently poor results. For example, in all 30 regions in Cook and Heizer's California study (1965, 1968), observed population values are less than one-half those predicted by the regression equation (2-1), and they are less than one-third the predicted value in all but five instances. Furthermore, the loglog regression equation obtained for their data (with population the dependent variable) is strikingly different:

$$\text{Predicted population} = 0.54994 \, (\text{floor area})^{0.62284}$$

Thus, whereas Naroll suggested that the relationship between floor area and population is nearly linear, Cook and Heizer found that California populations varied more nearly as the square root of floor area.

Refinement of Naroll's formula is definitely required if it is to become a credible research tool. But even if floor area were a perfect predictor of population, the purely archeological sources of error mentioned previously remain to be controlled.

One solution to the problem of delineating houses is to consider instead the relationship of total settlement area to population size. This can be expected to limit some of the problems arising from noncontemporaneity of the structures at a site. Regionally, a linear relationship between log (settlement area) and log (population size) is likely to be found. A linear relationship was confirmed between log (settlement area) and log (house count) in trials for a number of historic Indian groups from California and Tierra del Fuego (Cook and Treganza 1950:231-233; Cook and Heizer 1965, 1968). However, Cook and Heizer also found pronounced interregional variation in the regression parameters. For the entire state of California, the correlation coefficient of log (settlement area) and log (population) was just +0.37, a value far too low to permit reliable prediction of one variable from the other. High correlations were obtained only within three smaller regions. (In contrast, the correlation of log [floor area] and log [population] remained high even when the entire state was treated as a single region.) The necessity of calibrating and applying a predictor based on the site areas within a small, homogeneous region reduces the likelihood that the

required ethnohistoric data on the relationship are available. Furthermore, the instability of the correlation makes projection into the distant past more hazardous.

Even if reliable estimates of village population size could be obtained, prospects for estimating regional population levels would remain poor. Projecting from the village to the regional level requires a chronology sufficiently refined to establish the contemporaneity of occupations, and nowhere in eastern North America has this been accomplished.

Environmental Carrying Capacity

Possibly the carrying capacity of a region under a given technology can be used to estimate population size. However, the feasibility of the approach is questionable on a number of grounds: (1) Because the wild food potential from the rivers, forests, and prairies of midwestern United States is much different and much reduced today in comparison with times prior to major European settlement, quantitative assessments of past productivity are reliable only on an order of magnitude basis. (2) Since exploitation of natural resources by man alters their abundance, one needs empirical information about an ecosystem not only in a pristine state, but also with man as one of its components. (3) Because resource potential is itself a variable over time, populations are limited by the availability of food during the leanest seasons and years rather than by its average abundance. The consequences of scarcity can be moderated by food storage, but it is difficult to *measure* the importance of food storage for a prehistoric population. Also, do the severest shortages, which would have the most effective limiting force on population size, occur on the order of every 5, 25, or 100 years?

A prehistoric estimate based solely on resource potential assumes that populations are regulated at a level close to the maximum possible use of resources. However, there are several reasons why populations will be less than the theoretical limit:

1. Because of exploitative inefficiencies, actual resource use must be less than potential productivity.

2. In the attempt to maintain optimal environments for themselves, individuals and groups are inevitably involved, overtly or covertly, in ecological competition. For example, to minimize the consequences of adverse fluctuations of resources, it is desirable to maintain access to a wider range

than is normally required. As a consequence of competition, some individuals or groups may have restricted access to, or be excluded from, certain resources, or they may even be exploited in the service of others. Some competitive process in societies are ranking, alliances, territoriality, and emigration. A "manager's" strategy for maintaining the largest possible human population is almost certainly not identical with the strategy for environmental optimization followed by individuals and groups within the population.

3. If food supply is elastic, rather than a fixed parameter, then population equilibria may be established at several levels even without changes in subsistence technology. Consider, for example, the model for an environment in which potential food sources vary widely in the effort needed to procure them (Asch, Ford, and Asch 1972:27-29). Population growth in such an environment necessitates greater reliance on less desirable food sources, and consequently requires more labor per capita. The ultimate limit to growth in this environment is the point at which the large energy input into subsistence activities nullifies the returns. Assuming the rates of recruitment and loss for the population are density-dependent, there seem to be no theoretical reasons against balance occurring at population levels below the maximum possible size. A number of ethnographic investigations of hunter-gatherers have found levels of exploitation well below the point of diminishing returns (Lee 1968; Woodburn 1968; McCarthy and McArthur 1960). For agricultural societies, Boserup (1965) points to the history of increasingly intensive land use in many regions as evidence for the elasticity of food supply. She maintains that "population growth is ... the independent variable which in its turn is a major factor determining agricultural developments" (1965:11). For a stationary population established below the level of maximum resource exploitation, growth will be renewed when any cultural change depresses the mortality rate (e.g., a change in infant feeding practices or an advance in disease control), increases fertility, or increases the net migration into the region. The new equilibrium resulting from subsequent density-dependent adjustments will then be at a higher level, and subsistence effort will be correspondingly more intensive.

Though correlations of population size and resource levels have been demonstrated within some regions (Birdsell 1953; Baumhoff 1963; Hainline 1965), the above assertions are not necessarily contradicted. Given relatively high cultural homogeneity and effective mechanisms for population dispersal, minimization of per capita labor input by dispersal throughout a region should result in populations that are proportionately adjusted to resource levels even when well below the level of maximum resource utilization.

James A. Brown (personal communication) has suggested that if the foregoing relationships exist, then in principle one could predict population levels from absolute or relative measures of resource abundance. The procedure would resemble that followed by Baumhoff (1963) in his study of aboriginal California populations. If one can determine the population levels in several regions from investigations of their burial populations (using methods described in this study) and if one obtains indices of resource abundance in each of these regions, then regression equations can be calculated to predict population size in other regions from the resource variables. In establishing the population-resource relationship, each sample region should encompass the territory exploited by at least one prehistoric group. But drawing boundaries for a single prehistoric group is a speculative exercise. Therefore, to gain the advantages of statistical smoothing in the computation of population density, each sample region should be large enough to contain several groups. Because of the large data requirements, this method is presently infeasible.

Man-Years

Regional versus local estimates

The size and distribution of burial populations, the quantity of food refuse at habitation sites, or the frequencies of other variables that are empirically correlated with "quantity of occupation" provide a basis for estimating the number of man-years lived at a site or within a region. The number, divided by the length of time that the skeletal material or refuse accumulated, gives mean population size. Use of the method is exemplified by Ascher's calculation (1959) of the protein represented by subsistence remains in a California shell midden (see Glassow 1967), by Howells' population estimates (1960) based on burials at Pecos Pueblo and the Late Archaic Indian Knoll site, and by Jamison's (1971) similar estimate for the Middle Woodland Albany mound group in Illinois.

Single-site estimates such as these all encounter a crucial problem: determining the length of time the remains accumulated. Ordinarily, this variable is as difficult to measure as population itself. In the lower Illinois Valley, for example, only two or three chronological Middle Woodland subdivisions can be distinguished with any confidence (Struever 1968b:158-169; Griffin 1970)—hardly a basis for determining initial and terminal dates of occupation of a site or of detecting intermittent use. Because of the confounding of population size and length of occupation in the variable of man-years, local population estimates are usually unreliable.

Estimates in this study pertain to mean population size in a large region over a period of several hundred years. In part, the regional focus came about as an evasion of the almost insoluble problem of determining the length of use or occupation for single sites. It permits one to work within a period whose upper and lower time boundaries are marked by distinctive changes in artifact styles and by the appearance or disappearance of certain artifact types. Consequently, burials and habitation debris usually can be assigned accurately to a span of time as long as the Middle Woodland period. Moreover, the *percentage* error in dating the length of a long period is much less than the percentage error in determining length of use for a single site, and it steadily diminishes with refinements of regional chronology. Of course, in moving from a local to a regional context, the relevance of a population measure changes, but regional studies are warranted regardless of the feasibility of local level estimates. Problems expected to be more serious at the regional level are poor preservation and the large-scale data requirement.

The significance of an estimate of *average* population levels will be influenced by the extent of population fluctuations. Present evidence suggests that the Middle Woodland population of the region was larger than its Early Woodland predecessor (Struever 1968b:226-227; Perino 1962) and smaller than its early Late Woodland successor (Struever personal communication; Perino 1962). If the directional change was substantial, then a Middle Woodland average would approximate the actual population for only a short timespan within the Middle Woodland period.

Possibly, as village locations changed, the lower Illinois Valley population fluctuated greatly, usually being much higher or much lower than the average and perhaps at times nonexistent. Detailed microstyle studies in ceramics would provide one means of assessing the stability of settlement locations in and adjacent to the lower Illinois Valley area.

Quantities of food remains

A regional population estimate based on quantities of food remains preserved at habitation sites will provide a lower limit for the population level. Incomplete preservation, particularly of plant foods, presents the foremost challenge to this method. Another problem is the unknown quantity of food eaten outside the habitation areas. From a random excavation sample, the total quantity of faunal and floral materials preserved in a site can be estimated, and their contribution in protein or food energy determined. Once these values have been obtained for several sites, it is possible to extrapolate the total amount of food remains at all sites in the region. Although the number of man-years represented by food remains will surely be much smaller than the true number of man-years, it nonetheless can serve as a check on estimates produced by other methods. In the lower Illinois Valley, the information required for this estimate should eventually accumulate as a by-product of excavations conducted for other reasons.

Mound survey method

The most promising methods for determining Middle Woodland population size in the lower Illinois Valley are based on information from the mortuary population. One approach, hereafter termed the "Mound Survey Method," estimates population size as—

$$\text{Population} = \frac{\text{total man-years}}{L} = \frac{M \times \bar{N} \times \bar{A}}{L} \quad (2\text{-}2)$$

where M is the number of Middle Woodland mound groups, $\bar{N}$ is the mean size of mound group burial populations, $\bar{A}$ is mean age at death in the burial populations, and L is the length of the Middle Woodland period.

Two assumptions underlie the formula: (1) Mound burials constitute virtually the entire Middle Woodland mortuary population, and (2) the man-years lived by a community may be determined by multiplying the size of the associated mortuary population by the mean age at death of its members.

Several lines of evidence are relevant to the first assumption: the direct evidence obtained by archeologists for the frequency of burial in habitation sites or other unmounded situations, indications of destructive mortuary practices such as cremation, and the detection of underrepresentation of one sex or of certain age groups in mound populations. These are supplemented by the implications of a recent cross-cultural survey of intrasocietal variability in the treatment of the dead and in the social correlates of differential mortuary behavior (Binford 1971). This study provides a basis for assessing the likelihood that a large fraction of the mortuary population did not receive mound burial and yet left none of the above kinds of evidence for their existence.

Superficially, the second assumption underlying the formula seems reasonable. However, the mathematical relationships of vital statistics reveal that the following premises are built into this calculation of man-years: (1) The prehistoric population size was stationary, except for certain fluctuations resulting from migration; (2) the age structure was stable, i.e., time-invariant; and (3) the population was closed to migration, or if migration did occur, there were no accompanying changes in age structure. The assumptions are ideal, and deviation from them in the prehistoric demographic situation is difficult—in some cases, impossible—to measure. Consequently, it is necessary to assess the sensitivity of a population estimate to deviations from these assumptions.

The small size and haphazard selection of the regional sample, obtained during 100 years of archeological investigations, is a source of error, and the destruction of mounds by natural and human agencies introduces additional biases. Consequently, one cannot explicitly measure the error variance associated with exact population estimates derived from this sample. In response to this problem, an attempt was made to determine safe minimum and maximum values for the variables of Equation (2-2) as a basis for specifying minimum and maximum values for population size.

Mound-village calibration method

In the "Mound-Village Calibration method," a regional estimate of the number of man-years lived is obtained indirectly. Ideally, one determines the number of man-years lived at habitation sites in a region from the frequency of a certain debris category that has been demonstrated to vary in proportion to man-years. Debris frequency is translated into man-years by examining selected habitation sites with associated mound groups. Debris frequency is measured at the village and man-years from the associated burial population.

Because the necessary data from mound group-habitation pairs in the lower Illinois Valley are lacking, I have employed a variant form of the method which led to an estimated maximum population value. Man-years represented by the burials of the Gibson-Klunk mound groups were determined. This burial population is the largest documented in the region; and its habitation site, The Gardens of Kampsville, is well above the average in area and richness. If the mean number of man-years lived at *each* Middle Woodland village in the lower Illinois Valley region were equal to that of The Gardens of Kampsville, the total number of man-years lived in the region would equal The Gardens of Kampsville's contribution times the number of village sites. But because The Gardens of Kampsville is almost certainly above average in the extensiveness of its occupation, this estimate of man-years leads to a maximum estimate of the regional population size.

3

The Demographic Structure

In this chapter, I examine the demographic structure of a Middle Woodland burial population (from the Gibson-Klunk mound group) and identify assumptions entering into demographic reconstructions based on mortuary data. The following objectives motivate this discussion:

To show how mortuary populations provide information about man-years lived by prehistoric communities. Exploration of the mathematical model for vital statistics reveals that several demographic assumptions, some of them largely untestable, underlie the computation of man-years from mortuary data. The likelihood that these assumptions introduce serious errors into the population estimate is evaluated.

To compute provisional values for vital statistics, under the assumption that the burial population represents a complete prehistoric community. Provisional values falling outside anticipated ranges derived from comparable populations will be construed, conservatively, as evidence that part of the community is missing from the burial population. In turn this would warn that the data may yield seriously underestimated population levels.

To obtain statistics for use in the population estimate. This assumes that the issues of reliability have been resolved favorably.

To show how a variety of vital statistics may be computed from prehistoric mortuary data. In the course of this study many vital statistics were evaluated for the clues they provide about completeness of the mortuary population. Moreover, the attention given to the demographic model laid bare many assumptions underlying their computation. This work has value not only as a means toward a more reliable population estimate but also as an exploration of the range of demographic information which, with varying degrees of reliability, may be computed from mortuary data. The following account of demographic structure is elaborated slightly beyond the minimal requirements for a population estimate in order to indicate the potential of several seldom-used paleodemographic statistics.

1. THE DEMOGRAPHIC MODEL

The published works of prehistoric demography have given little attention to the assumptions underlying the calculation of vital statistics, assumptions which should be explicit because the level of confidence in demographic reconstruction depends on their credibility. For example, I assumed at first that the number of man-years lived by a community during a given time interval is the product of two measurable variables: the size of the mortuary population accumulating during that interval and the mean age at death. Unfortunately, this is true only for special cases, e.g., under the dual conditions of zero population growth and a stable age structure.

Therefore, to determine the relationship between man-years and accessible mortality statistics, and to show how other vital statistics can be obtained from mortality data, a formal mathematical model for population growth and structure was applied—a model explicitly formulating the relationships of population size, natality, mortality, and changes through time. This model for vital statistics is, for convenience, termed the *demographic model,* though by no means does it consider all demographic variables. It has been formulated and elaborated for many years, Alfred J. Lotka (1939) being perhaps the most notable of the pioneers. Two excellent recent discussions are *Introduction to the Mathematics of Population* (Keyfitz 1968) and *The Concept of a Stable Population* (United Nations 1968). I am dependent on these publications for the basic definitions and formulas presented in this paper.*

Since the demographic model does not permit a reconstruction of vital statistics solely from knowl-

---

*Since the completion of this study, an excellent monograph by K. M. Weiss (1973) has been published, which discusses demographic models in application to primitive and prehistoric populations.

edge of the age distribution and size of a burial population, assumptions must be introduced if mortuary populations are to be tapped as a source of demographic information. One useful restriction in the model is to assume a stable, i.e., unchanging age structure; another is to employ a specific rate of population growth. The validity of these assumptions is difficult to assess in specific archeological contexts. However, it may still be possible to ascertain a range of error for computed statistics if the domain of reasonable values for uncontrolled variables can be specified.

Definitions of Vital Statistics

Even though changes of population are integer-valued functions, the demographic model is defined for a set of continuous variables because "functions of continuous variables are the principal means of looking more deeply into age at death and many other demographic matters" (Keyfitz 1968:5).

For readers not acquainted with the integral notation employed in the following sections, a brief explanation is provided in Appendix A. In addition, at the end of each section most of the mathematical expressions using integrals are restated in discrete form. These are identified by the same index numbers as their integral equivalents. For instance, Equation (3-3′) is the discrete counterpart of (3-3).

The notation requires some prefatory comments:

—Symbols for variables have the same meaning when they occur in both discrete and integral equations.

—When reference is made to age intervals $(a, a+n)$, the age distribution may be divided into intervals of differing width n. Where confusion might otherwise result, width is explicitly identified as a variable by using the notation n_a.

—The midpoint of the interval $(a, a+n)$ is denoted by

$$a' = a + \tfrac{1}{2}n$$

—The limits of summation are to be interpreted loosely as meaning that the sum is to be taken over all age intervals defined within the specified range.

These discrete approximations are used in the actual computations of vital statistics. A presentation of the demographic model entirely in terms of discrete variables may be found in Barclay (1958).

Population size and the size of age classes.—Let K = population size. As a variable through time,

the population at time t can be symbolized by the functional notation $K(t)$. The graph in Figure 3 illustrates the notation used to represent the size of age classes. Age a is the abscissa of the graph and a variable $k(a)$ is the ordinate, defined to have the following properties: (1) The total area under the curve and above the a-axis represents population size K; (2) between any two ages a and β, the area under the curve (i.e., the shaded region of the graph) represents the number of individuals within that age class. Thus, $k(a)\,da$ is the number of individuals within the age interval $(a, a + da)$; the integral

$$\int_a^\beta k(a)\,da \qquad (3\text{-}1)$$

gives the size of the age class between ages a and β; and the size of the entire population is

$$K = \int_0^\omega k(a)\,da \qquad (3\text{-}2)$$

where ω is the maximum age at death.

Age structure.—The proportion of the total population in the age class with upper and lower boundaries a and $a + da$ is represented by

$$c(a)\,da = \frac{k(a)\,da}{\int_0^\omega k(x)\,dx} = \frac{k(a)\,da}{K}$$

For a more tangible age class between ages a and β, the proportion is given by the integral

$$\int_a^\beta c(a)\,da = \frac{\int_a^\beta k(a)\,da}{K} \qquad (3\text{-}3)$$

Cohort.—A cohort is defined as a group of individuals born at the same time; i.e., during the interval t to $t + dt$. When actual data are used, a cohort refers to a group born over a small but measurable timespan, for example, a 1-year period.

Survivorship.—Suppose that a cohort consists of $l(0)$ individuals at birth; a years later there are $l(a)$ survivors; at maximum age ω, there are no survivors: $l(\omega) = 0$. The life history of a cohort is thus summarized by a plot of $l(a)$ versus a. Survivorship is often standardized in terms of an arbitrary initial cohort size such as 1,000 or 100,000; so that $l(a)$ represents survivorship per 1,000, per 100,000, or some other base. An example is the estimated survivorship curve for the population producing the burials of the Gibson-Klunk mound groups (see Fig. 7, p. 33).

A survivorship curve is often presented in terms of the *proportion* $p(a)$ of all individuals surviving to age a. Obviously,

$$p(a) = \frac{l(a)}{l(0)} \qquad (3\text{-}4)$$

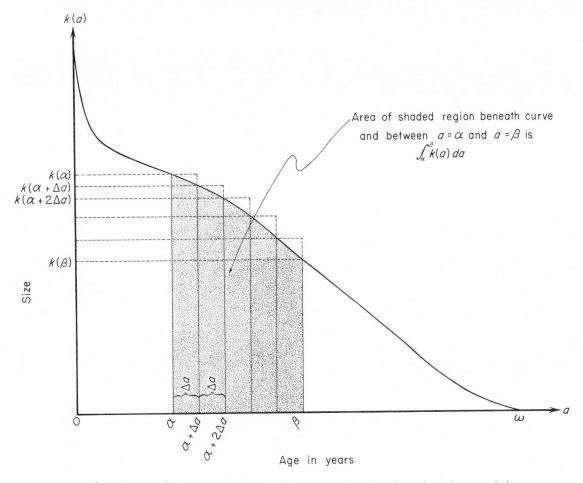

Figure 3. Definition of the continuous variable $k(a)$ representing size of age classes in a population.

and $p(0) = 1$. Now consider a new variable $p*(a)$, defined as the *prior probability* that a randomly selected member of a cohort survives to age a. The *expected value* of the percentage of a cohort surviving to age a also equals $p*(a)$. In small populations, "chance variations" often cause observed survivorship $p(a)$ to deviate considerably from the survival probability $p*(a)$. However, large populations normally give nearly identical values of $p(a)$ and $p*(a)$; then, $p(a)$ denotes, approximately, an observed survivorship percentage, a probability, or an expected value. In this paper, the percentage and probability of survival are treated as if they were identical.

In a population observed at time t each age group belongs to a different cohort; i.e., the group of age a belongs to the cohort born at time $t - a$. The probabilities of survival can and, in general, do vary from one cohort to another.

Mortality.—An *age-specific mortality rate* is the limiting value of the death rate as the time interval becomes very small. It is symbolized by $\mu(a)$ and defined as

$$\mu(a) = \frac{1}{l(a)} \left(-\frac{dl(a)}{da} \right) \qquad (3\text{-}5)$$

that is, $\mu(a)$ is the instantaneous rate of decline in the cohort at age a, standardized for the number of survivors at that age (i.e., a per capita rate). For large populations $\mu(a)\, da$ can also be interpreted either as the observed percentage of survivors to age a who die before attaining age $a + da$ or as the probability of a person of age a dying before age $a + da$.

Suppose, hypothetically, that between ages a and $\beta = a + n$ the mortality rate has a constant value represented by $_n\mu_a$. Then it can be shown that survivorship at age $a + n$ is

$$l(a + n) = l(a)e^{-n\mu_a n}$$

(This is an example of the exponential law of decay; it is formally identical to the function describing the decay of radioactive isotopes; e is the base of natural logarithms, equal to 2.71828 approximately.) If the mortality rate is a variable $\mu(a)$, as must be true in general, then the exponent $_n\mu_a n$ must be replaced by the integral $\int_a^{a+n}\mu(a)\, da$. The value of this integral equals the mean mortality rate $_n\bar\mu_a$ between ages a and $a + n$ times the width of the age interval. Thus, an alternative form of the relationship is

$$l(a + n) = l(a)e^{-n\bar\mu_a n} \qquad (3\text{-}6)$$

Solving for the mean mortality rate gives

$$_n\bar\mu_a = \frac{\ln l(a) - \ln l(a + n)}{n} \qquad (3\text{-}7)$$

(The symbol ln stands for "natural logarithm.")

It also follows that the survival probability $p(a)$ and the age-specific mortality rate are related by

$$p(a) = \exp\left[-\int_0^a \mu(x)\, dx\right] \qquad (3\text{-}8)$$

Life expectancy.—At age a the mean number of years remaining to members of a cohort is equal to the total man-years still to be lived by them, divided by the cohort size at that age. Graphically (see Fig. 7) life expectancy at age a is the area under the $l(a)$ curve to the right of a, divided by $l(a)$, or

$$\mathcal{e}(a) = \frac{\int_a^\omega l(x)\, dx}{l(a)} \qquad (3\text{-}9)$$

Fertility.—The *age-specific fertility* of women $m(a)$ is a continuous function, where $m(a)\, da$ is defined as the percentage of women giving birth to a female child when they are between the ages of a and $a + da$. For large populations, $m(a)\, da$ may also be considered a probability.

The *age distribution of fertility* $F(a)$ among the female members of a population is defined as

$$F(a)\, da = \frac{m(a)\, da}{\int_u^v m(x)\, dx} \qquad (3\text{-}10)$$

where u and v are, respectively, the lower and upper limits of the childbearing age.

Gross reproduction rate R' is a measure of the total fertility (female births) of women in a population, without adjustment for population age structure. It is defined as

$$R' = \int_u^v m(a)\, da \qquad (3\text{-}11)$$

Crude birth and death rates and rate of population growth.—By *crude birth rate b* is meant the birth rate for the entire population, male and female. It is the limiting value of the birth rate as the time interval becomes very short. The *crude death rate d* is defined similarly, and the rate of population increase is simply

$$r = b - d$$

Discrete counterparts for integral notation

Let $_nK_a$ (3-1') be the number of individuals between the ages of a and $a+n$ years; let $_nK_a(t)$ be the same statistic, referenced to a specific time t. Total population size K is, of course,

$$K = \sum_{a=0}^\omega {}_nK_a \qquad (3\text{-}2')$$

The proportion $_nC_a$ of the population that is between the ages of a and $a+n$ is

$$_nC_a = \frac{_nK_a}{K} \qquad (3\text{-}3')$$

The survival probability $p(a)$ and the age specific mortality rate $_n\bar\mu_a$ are related by

$$p(a) \doteqdot \exp\left(-\sum_{x=0}^a {}_n\bar\mu_x n\right) \qquad (3\text{-}8')$$

Life expectancy $\mathcal{e}(a)$ at age a is approximately

$$\mathcal{e}(a) \doteqdot \frac{\sum_{x=a}^\omega n l(x')}{l(a)} \qquad (3\text{-}9')$$

where x' is, successively, the midpoint $x + \tfrac{1}{2}n$ of age groups $(x, x+n)$.

Let the variable $_nF_a$ represent the proportion of a woman's total reproductive contribution expected during age interval $(a, a + n_a)$. Assuming that within age groups $m(a)$ is nearly constant,

$$_nF_a \doteqdot \frac{n_a m(a')}{\sum_{x=u}^v n_x m(x')} \qquad (3\text{-}10')$$

The gross reproduction rate R' is, approximately,

$$R' \doteqdot \sum_{a=u}^v n m(a') \qquad (3\text{-}11')$$

The Concept of a Stable Population

One of the most useful special cases of the demographic model assumes that mortality and fertility rates $\mu(a)$ and $m(a)$ are constant from one cohort to the next; i.e., they do not change through time though they may vary with age. It can be proved that the maintenance of this condition over a period of many years results in a constant rate r of population increase or decrease or of zero growth, termed the *intrinsic* or *Malthusian* rate of increase (Keyfitz 1968:89-90). Also, b and d remain constant. Age structures $c(a)$ and survival probabilities $p(a)$, though they vary with age, do not change through time. Such populations are termed *stable* because the proportion of the population within an age class does not change. By this definition, a stable population can nonetheless be either growing or declining. When in addition to stability no change in size occurs ($r = 0$), the population is said to be *stationary*.

Some important relationships in a stable population are

$$K(t) = e^{rt}K(0) \qquad (3\text{-}12)$$

indicating an exponential rate of population growth or decline;

$$b = \frac{1}{\int_0^\omega e^{-ra}p(a)\,da} \qquad (3\text{-}13)$$

birth rate expressed as a function of survivorship probabilities and rate of population growth;

$$c(a)\,da = \frac{e^{-ra}p(a)\,da}{\int_0^\omega e^{-rx}p(x)\,dx} \qquad (3\text{-}14)$$

age structure expressed as a function of survivorship probabilities and the rate of population growth; and

$$\int_u^v e^{-ra}p(a)m(a)\,da = 1 \qquad (3\text{-}15)$$

which relates the age-specific mortality and fertility rates of women under a known range of population growth. Note that given r and the set of $p(a)$, the set of $m(a)$ that satisfies the equation is *not* uniquely determined.

Discrete counterparts for integral notation

The discrete forms for some important relationships among vital statistics in stable populations are

$$b \doteq \frac{1}{\sum_{a=0}^\omega ne^{-ra'}p(a')} \qquad (3\text{-}13')$$

$$_nC_a \doteq \frac{n_a e^{-ra'}p(a')}{\sum_{x=0}^\omega n_x e^{-rx'}p(x')} \qquad (3\text{-}14')$$

and

$$\sum_{a=u}^v ne^{-ra'}p(a')m(a') \doteq 1 \qquad (3\text{-}15')$$

Independent Variables of the Demographic Model

Mortality rates $\mu(a)$ or $p(a)$ and fertility rates $m(a)$ are the basic variables of the demographic model because, for a stable population, they determine crude birth and death rates, the per capita rate of population change, and the age structure. No other two-variable combination in this set is sufficient to determine all the remaining ones.

For instable populations, the list of basic variables must be expanded to include the age structure $c(a)\,da$ at some arbitrary origin time t_0 for the analysis, and the other variables must be treated as functions of time t. Variables determining the state of the instable system are thus

$$K(0),\ c(a, t_0),\ \mu(a, t),\ m(a, t),\ \text{and } t$$

Inclusion of t as an independent variable expresses the fact that age structure, crude birth and death rates, and rates of population growth vary through time except in the case of stability.

Three other fundamental variables should be recognized: (1) drift, (2) migration, and (3) sex ratio.

Drift takes into account the inexact aspect of the correspondence of mortality and fertility rates with their probabilities. Large percentage deviations of the observed rates from the true probabilities are likely to occur in small populations; when the probabilities themselves are estimated from population data, the estimated and true values will in general differ. Drift is a major obstacle to the application of the deterministic form of the demographic model to very small populations for which considerably more complex stochastic models may be required. However, if the population under study can be redefined by enlarging the spatial boundaries, then the larger size of the new population will minimize the effect of drift.

A second variable is migration. The relationships thus far described pertain to populations closed to migration. Virilocal and uxorilocal residence patterns do not seriously violate the closed population assumption, since the resulting immigration and emigration should tend to be balanced, with no net changes in the age-sex composition of the community. If the community age structure is left unchanged and the migrant and sedentary subpopulations have the same age-specific fertility and mortality rates, then the vital statistics, including mean population size, can be calculated as if the population were closed, even for communities in which migration leads to fluctuations in size.

The third variable is the sex ratio, which in many cases can be treated as a constant or assumed approximately equal to 1.

2. DEMOGRAPHY OF THE BURIAL POPULATION

From the demographic model, several vital statistics can be estimated for the Middle Woodland burials of the Gibson and Pete Klunk mound groups. Being the most carefully excavated mounds with the most extensively analyzed skeletal series in the region, they are the primary source of information about the demographic structure of Middle Woodland populations.

Evidence is also reviewed concerning the likelihood that the Gibson-Klunk burials represent the entire mortuary population of a community. Burial in other locations and destruction of skeletal remains by prehistoric mortuary practices or by natural processes are potential causes of under-representation. If the pattern of exclusion from a burial population does not alter the age and sex proportions, then estimates of birth and death rates and of community age structure are unaffected, though statistics functionally related to population size will be inaccurate. But more often an incompletely represented mortuary population can be expected to have biased age-sex proportions. The procedure of this paper is first to calculate Gibson-Klunk statistics as if the entire population were represented and then to evaluate the results with respect to theoretical predictions grounded in human biology or to expectations for populations lacking effective control of disease. From this investigation may come a decision not to use the statistics or an attempt to correct frequencies of some age classes or of the minority sex.

Assuming that the entire population is represented, evidence is then presented that the simple formula

Man-years = (size of burial population)
× (mean age of death)

serves as an adequate *approximation* for the purposes of this population estimate.

The acceptability of an estimate of man-years or any other vital statistic is, of course, partly a function of the intended use of the estimate. Thus, the decision to use the Gibson-Klunk statistics in the population estimate does not imply that they

may be employed safely for other purposes. Furthermore, the vital statistics that were computed are not equally reliable. For example, inferences concerning fertility are less directly determined from the primary data—the age distribution of the burial population—than are age-specific mortality rates, and the crude death rate is highly influenced by assumptions about the rate of population growth.

The reliability of a prehistoric vital statistic cannot be measured objectively, at least not without numerous qualifying assumptions. However, with the demographic model one can assess the "distance"—i.e., the number and strength of intervening assumptions—between the empirical input and the statistic. Moreover, the model can be manipulated by using trial values for the uncontrolled variables in order to observe the sensitivity of the estimated statistic to these sources of error. Consequences of deviation from stability can often be specified; *The Concept of a Stable Population* (United Nations 1968) has an excellent discussion of this matter.

Sex Ratio

A strongly imbalanced sex ratio among the Gibson-Klunk burials would imply that they do not represent a complete mortuary population. However, such is not the case. Among post-adolescent individuals, Buikstra (1972) identified 169 males and 168 females from the two groups. Gibson yielded 46 males and 45 females and the Pete Klunk mounds 123 males and 123 females. Clearly no large sex differential exists.

Evaluation of Age

Most of the demographic information for the Gibson-Klunk burials was obtained from the distribution of age at death. Age evaluations for the entire Gibson population and for most of the Pete Klunk burials were provided to me by Jane Buikstra (see Buikstra 1972 for her criteria). Another evaluation of the Klunk Hopewell population, by King B. Hunter, has been published (Blakely 1971), and Buikstra consulted Hunter's notes before making her final age assessments. Buikstra's reexamination of the skeletal series, including incompletely represented individuals, increased the estimated population at Klunk by about 20 percent.

Lest spurious interpretations arise from the uncertainties of age evaluation, a discussion of the

Gibson-Klunk age structure must consider the reliability of age determinations based on skeletal material. As Buikstra (1972:25) observes, "the accuracy of biological age evaluations varies inversely with the maturity of the skeleton." Thus, while the age of an infant usually can be determined to within a few months, a well-preserved skeleton of a mature adult is often impossible to place within a 5-year range. Therefore, Buikstra stated the age of each individual in terms of a range rather than as an exact estimate. Incomplete and poorly preserved skeletons constituting a substantial minority of the Gibson-Klunk population were specified only as *infant* (0-3 years), *child* (3-12 years), *adolescent* (12-18 years), *subadult* (18-21 years), *young adult* (21-35 years), *middle adult* (35-50 years), or *old adult* (50+ years). After age 50, reliable age discriminations are difficult or impossible to make even for well-preserved skeletons. Consequently, old adult skeletons have not been subdivided into narrower age categories. Some Pete Klunk mound group skeletons were unavailable for laboratory study and were classified by field observations as either children or adults, no finer discrimination being generally possible. Buikstra was unable to examine a few other individuals in the Klunk series whose ages had previously been assessed to the nearest year by Hunter. Ages of three individuals excavated by Middleton from the Pete Klunk mound group were not evaluated. (See Chap. 4, Sect. 2.)

For the population estimate, the age distribution was divided into 1-year classes up to age 3 and by 5-year classes between ages 5 and 50. In cases where the age range given for a burial overlapped my classes, it was assigned to these classes by the two techniques of proportionate allocation described below:

Age range overlapped two age classes.—Each age class was allocated a fraction of an individual equal to the proportion of the individual's age range overlapping the age class. For example, a skeleton 42 to 47 years old was allocated to the 40 to 44.99 year age class and to the 45 to 49.99 year age class and was considered as a contribution of 0.6 and 0.4 individual, respectively, to the two classes.

Age range overlapped more than two age classes.—First, except for those individuals with the widest age ranges, all members of the burial population were assigned to age classes. Let us suppose that the initial age distribution for ages 35 to 50 is

35 to 39.99 years: 36 individuals
40 to 44.99 years: 48 individuals
45 to 49.99 years: 66 individuals

and that 10 other individuals are classified only as middle-age adults (35 to 50 years). Then $10 \times 36/(36+48+66) = 2.4$ individuals are added to the 35 to 39.99 year age class, $10 \times 48/150 = 3.2$ are added to the 40 to 44.99 year age class, and 4.4 individuals are added to the 45 to 49.99 year age class, giving a revised age distribution of

35 to 39.99 years: 38.4 individuals
40 to 44.99 years: 51.2 individuals
45 to 49.99 years: 70.4 individuals

Individuals thus added do not change the relative frequencies among the age classes they overlap, but they do increase the size of these age classes with respect to all others.

The resulting age distribution does not exactly replicate that reported by Buikstra (1972) because she was more conservative in using the data for individuals assigned to broad age classes in the field and because of minor differences in the procedure for allocating burials whose age ranges overlapped the arbitrary age classes.

Age Distribution

The age distribution of the Gibson-Klunk burial population is graphed in Figure 4A and tabulated in Table 3, column 2 (p. 32). An impressionistic comparison with theoretical frequency curves for age at death permits some weak inferences about possible age group bias. Probably all human populations have age-specific mortality curves of the shape illustrated in Figure 5A, for there are underlying biological reasons why life should be more precarious for the very young and the very old (Caughley 1966). In a stationary population, the actual number of deaths recorded for any age will resemble one of the curves of Figure 5B. In a growing population, younger individuals are relatively more numerous, and the number of deaths —not the death rate—will increase toward the younger end of the age scale. Conversely, a declining population will accentuate deaths of older individuals.

The Gibson-Klunk age distribution roughly resembles the hypothetical distributions of death illustrated in Figure 5B. Lack of correspondence to the hypothetical case is most pronounced between ages 25 and 50, but some improvement results from replotting ages 20 to 50 in 10-year intervals. Possibly the unevenness of the empirical

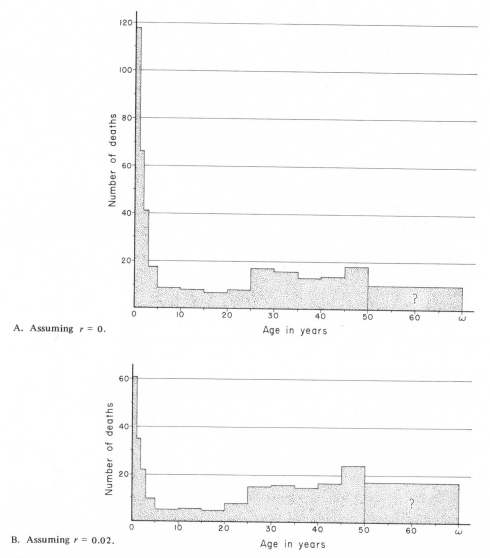

A. Assuming *r* = 0.

B. Assuming *r* = 0.02.

Figure 4. Age distribution of the Gibson-Klunk burial population and of deaths within a cohort—standardized to 1,000 deaths and assuming a stable age structure. Maximal age ω is arbitrarily set at 70 years.

curve from one age class to the next is caused by small-sample variation and the uncertainties in age evaluation rather than by cultural selection against interment of specific age classes in the mounds. It may also be significant that the unevenness is greatest for adults, for which divergence of chronological age from biological age is most likely to occur.

At first disregarding the possibility of underrepresentation at this juncture, vital statistics for the living prehistoric population represented by the Gibson-Klunk burials will be estimated from these age distributions. This leads to a decision

point: If the resulting statistics seem unreasonable for a population lacking knowledge of disease control, one may decide not to use them in making a population estimate or may attempt a correction for underrepresentation.

Necessary Assumptions

The general version of the demographic model —with information about age distribution and size of burial population—does not permit a reconstruction of vital statistics. Date of death, too, must be known; and it being a datum rarely ascertainable in archeological situations, it be-

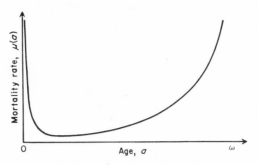

A. Generalized graph of age-specific mortality rates.

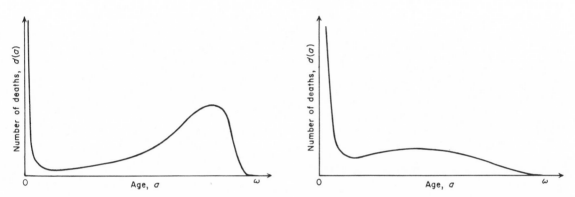

B. Possible distributions of number of deaths by age, given mortality rate curves of a shape similar to the generalized graph.

Figure 5. Generalized age-specific mortality rates and age distribution of deaths for human populations.

comes necessary to postulate a stable population and to choose an arbitrary value of *r*, the growth rate (Carrier 1958; Caughley 1966).

Errors due to the assumption of stability are difficult to assess. One justification for using the stable model is that vital statistics (except for absolute size) approach constant values if age-specific fertility and mortality rates do not fluctuate. Another justification is based upon the convergence of average values of statistics over long time periods to the statistics of the stable case. However, at the least, one should be alert for archeological evidence of catastrophic mortality, which would invalidate the assumption. Also, the assumption is less defensible if other evidence— e.g., major subsistence changes—suggests that demographic instability is likely within the time-span of the estimates.

If the stable model is used, there remains the problem of selecting a value for *r*. Two reconstructions are presented, one for *r* = 0 (a stationary population) and one for continuous growth at a rate of *r* = 0.02 per year. A comparison of these special cases will suggest the level of uncertainty resulting from lack of information about the growth rate.

As an alternative to the following presentation of vital statistics calculable from the age distribution of deaths, the reader may refer to Carrier (1958) or to *The Concept of a Stable Population* (United Nations 1968:14,17).

The Stationary Case (*r* = 0)

Relationship of age distribution of burials to cohort deaths

Assuming stability, it follows that age-specific mortality and fertility rates and survival probabilities do not vary among cohorts. Age structure and crude birth and death rates also remain constant during the accumulation time of the burial population. In short, these variables are time-independent under stability.

Assuming a stationary size and knowing only the age structure of the burial population, values can be calculated for all the vital statistics used in this paper except man-years, population size, and age-specific fertility rates. It will be shown that neither population size nor the period of accumulation is necessary for these computations. To calculate the man-years lived by a prehistoric population during a certain time interval, one must also know the size of the mortuary population of that interval. Not only the size and age structure of the mortuary population but also the timespan during which it accumulated must be determined before the population size of a prehistoric community can be obtained.

The first step in reconstruction is to derive a survivorship curve $l(a)$ from the age distribution of the mortuary population. However, this requires further exploration of relationships among demographic variables in the stationary case. Four assertions relate burial statistics and $l(a)$:

1. In a stable population—whether it be growing, stationary, or declining—the unvarying age structure and constant age-specific mortality rates imply that the proportion of deaths occurring at a specific age among deaths at all ages is also time-invariant.
2. Hence, the age structure of the entire mortuary population is identical to the age distribution of deaths for any moment of time $(t, t + dt)$.
3. The age distribution of deaths in a population, viewed synchronically at an arbitrary time $(t, t + dt)$, duplicates the cohort death history.
4. Consequently, *a burial population may be regarded as if it were a single cohort of individuals.*

Proof of Assertion 1 is given in Appendix B, Statement 1. The proportion of all deaths occurring at a specific age also remains constant in populations open to migration provided the community age structure is unaffected. If the size of such a community is affected only by migration, the community can be studied as if it were closed and stationary.

Assertion 2 follows directly from Assertion 1. Thus, a burial population preserves a synchronic record of mortality in the prehistoric community.

However, to calculate a survivorship curve, a history of deaths for *cohorts* is required: Hence, Assertions 3 and 4 are made. Assertion 4 is true if the previous assertions are valid.

A formal proof of Assertion 3, the identity between the synchronic age-specific structure of deaths and cohort death history, is easily constructed (see App. B, Statement 2). In the text, I present an intuitive and geometrical argument for the identity by comparing the age distribution of deaths during a hypothetical 1-year period with the diachronic record of death for the members of any of the population's cohorts born over a 1-year period. The history of the cohort born during year t is represented schematically in Figure 6 by the shaded region sloping at a 45° angle, and the synchronic record for the stationary population considered during year t lies within the horizontal shaded region. It is necessary to show that between ages a and $a + 1$, the number of deaths among the cohort *born* during year t and in the population *living* during year t are equal. For example, in the third-year age class, deaths in the square $EFGH$ of Figure 6 must equal deaths in the parallelogram $ABCD$. This is true of stationary populations for the following reasons:

1. The vital statistics of the subpopulation within $\triangle EGH$ (i.e., the history during year t of the subpopulation whose second birthday occurred during year t) are identical to those for the subpopulation in $\triangle ABD$ (i.e., the history during year $t + 2$ of the subpopulation whose second birthday occurred during year $t + 2$) since population size and age structure are invariant through time.
2. Similarly, the vital statistics of the individuals in $\triangle EFG$ (i.e., the history during year t of the subpopulation which was between 2 and 3 years old at the beginning of the year) are identical to those for $\triangle DBC$ (i.e., the history during year $t + 3$ of the subpopulation between 2 and 3 years old at the beginning of the year).
3. Therefore (deaths in $\square EFGH$) = (deaths in $\triangle EGH$) + (deaths in $\triangle EFG$) = (deaths in $\triangle ABD$) + (deaths in $\triangle DBC$) = (deaths in $\square ABCD$).

Having shown that the mortuary population can be examined for the stationary case as if it represented a single cohort, estimates of the Gibson-Klunk vital statistics can now be obtained. It is convenient to work with a cohort of arbitrary size, such that the absolute number of deaths at a given age in the burial population equals the number of deaths occurring at the same age in the cohort.

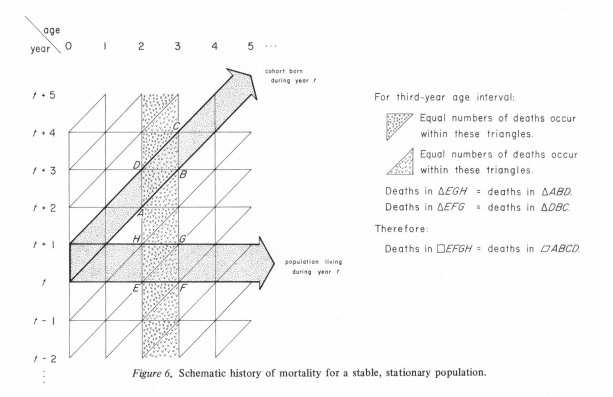

Figure 6. Schematic history of mortality for a stable, stationary population.

By definition, at age ω all individuals in the cohort have died.

Those that died during age $\omega - 1$ may be written as

$$_1D_{\omega-1} = \int_{\omega-1}^{\omega} D(a)\, da$$

where $D(a)\, da$ represents the number of individuals in the burial population between ages a and $a + da$. (For $r = 0$, it is also the number of deaths occurring at this age in the arbitrary cohort.) Then $_1D_{\omega-1}$ must have survived to their $(\omega-1)$th birthdays. If $_1D_{\omega-2}$ died at age $\omega-2$, then $_1D_{\omega-1} + \,_1D_{\omega-2}$ survived to their $(\omega-2)$th birthdays. In general, let

$$l(a) = \sum_{j=a}^{\omega} {_1D_j} = \int_a^{\omega} D(x)\, dx \qquad (3\text{-}16)$$

be the number reaching ath birthday, where the $_1D_j$-values are taken from the number of individuals of that age in the burial population. Therefore, the arbitrary initial cohort size $l(0)$ equals the total size D of the burial population:

$$l(0) = D = \sum_{j=0}^{\omega} {_1D_j} = \int_0^{\omega} D(a)\, da \qquad (3\text{-}17)$$

Similarly, the proportion surviving to the ath birthday is

$$p(a) = \frac{\sum_{j=a}^{\omega} {_1D_j}}{D} = \frac{\int_a^{\omega} D(x)\, dx}{D}$$

Statement 2 of Appendix B proves that, given the definition of $l(0)$ in Equation (3-17), survivorship at age a in the cohort is in fact expressed by Equation (3-16).

Vital statistics for Gibson-Klunk (r = 0)

For the Gibson-Klunk burial population, 106.8 individuals lived to age 50, 106.8 + 47.6 = 154.4 reached age 45, etc. Table 3 is a life table providing statistics for this population. Column 3 lists the survivorship in the arbitrary cohort; 533 individuals constitute the initial size of the arbitrary cohort. Survival probabilities are recorded in column 4, and age-specific mortality rates, obtained from Equation (3-7), are given in column 10.

Using Equation (3-14), we can calculate the percentage of the population within any age interval; for example, between ages a and β.

TABLE 3. *Life Table for the Gibson-Klunk Burial Population, Assuming Stability and Zero Growth Rate (r = 0)*

(1)	(2)	(3)	(4)	(5)	(6)	(7)	(8)	(9)	(10)	(11)
					Model 1: ω = 70 years		Model 2: ω = 80 years			
Age in years a	Number of deaths within age interval $(a,a+n)$ $\int_a^{a+n} D(a)\,da$	Survivorship $l(a)$	Survival probability $p(a)$	Man-years lived during age interval $(a,a+n)$ by all of burial pop. $\int_a^{a+n} l(a)\,da$	Proportion of living pop. within age interval $(a,a+n)$ $\int_a^{a+n} c(a)\,da$	Proportion of living pop. less than age a $\int_0^a c(a)\,da$	Proportion of living pop. within age interval $(a,a+n)$ $\int_a^{a+n} c(a)\,da$	Proportion of living pop. less than age a $\int_0^a c(a)\,da$	Annual mortality rate $_n\bar\mu_a$	Age in years a
0	62.6	533	1	501.7	⎫ 0.141	0	⎫ 0.136	0	0.1249	0
1	35.1	470.4	.833	452.8	⎪	.032	⎪	.031	⎫	1
2	21.7	435.3	.817	424.5	⎬	.061	⎬	.059	⎬ .0435	2
3	18.3	413.6	.776	808.9	⎭	.089	⎭	.086	⎭	3
5	22.4	395.3	.742	1,920.5	.123	.141	.119	.136	.0117	5
10	21.1	372.9	.700	1,811.7	.116	.264	.113	.255	.0116	10
15	17.7	351.8	.660	1,714.8	.110	.381	.107	.368	.0103	15
20	21.6	334.1	.627	1,616.5	⎫ .197	.491	⎫ .191	.474	.0134	20
25	45.2	312.5	.586	1,449.5	⎭	.595	⎭	.575	.0312	25
30	41.6	267.3	.502	1,232.5	⎫ .146	.688	⎫ .141	.665	.0338	30
35	35.3	225.7	.423	1,040.2	⎭	.767	⎭	.742	.0340	35
40	36.0	190.4	.357	862.0	⎫ .097	.834	⎫ .091	.806	.0419	40
45	47.6	154.4	.290	653.0	⎭	.889	⎭	.860	.0737	45
50	106.8	106.8	.200	(?)	⎫ .069	.931	⎫ .100	.900	—	50
ω	—	0	0	—	⎭	1	⎭	1	—	ω

$\Sigma = 533$
= size of burial pop.

Model 1: $\Sigma = 15,556.6$
Model 2: $\Sigma = 16,090.6$

Note: In discrete notation, columns 2, 5, 6 (and 8), and 7 (and 9) are, respectively, $_nD_a$, $_nL_a$, $_nC_a$ and $\sum_{x=0}^{a} {_nC_x}$.

$$\int_a^\beta c(a)\,da = \frac{\int_a^\beta e^{-0\cdot a}p(a)\,da}{\int_0^\omega e^{-0\cdot a}p(a)\,da} = \frac{\int_a^\beta p(a)\,da}{\int_0^\omega p(a)\,da}$$

or since $l(a) = l(0)p(a)$,

$$\int_a^\beta c(a)\,da = \frac{\int_a^\beta l(a)\,da}{\int_0^\omega l(a)\,da} \qquad (3\text{-}18)$$

That is, the fraction of the population between a and β years old equals the area under the curve of $l(a)$ between a and β, divided by the total area beneath the survivorship curve (Fig. 7).

The area between a and β (Fig. 7) is approximately

$$\int_a^\beta l(a)\,da \doteq l(\beta)(\beta-a)+\tfrac{1}{2}\left[l(a)-l(\beta)\right](\beta-a)$$

$$= \tfrac{1}{2}\left[l(a)+l(\beta)\right](\beta-a) \qquad (3\text{-}19)$$

For example, the area between 30 and 35 years under the survivorship curve for the Gibson-Klunk cohort is $\tfrac{1}{2}(267.3 + 225.7)(5) = 1{,}232.5$ man-years (Table 3, column 5). This represents the total number of years lived between ages 30 and 35 by members of the burial population or by the hypothetical cohort.

A complicating factor in determining the number of years lived by all 533 members of the burial population or cohort is that deaths above the age of 50 are not assigned to age classes. We therefore provide two reconstructions: (1) Model 1, which is based on the constant decline of the 50+ survivors with $\omega = 70$ years, and (2) Model 2, which is based on the constant decline until $\omega = 80$. For Model 1, $\int_{50}^{70}l(a)\,da = 1{,}068.0$ man-years, and the total man-years lived by the cohort is estimated as 15,556.6. For Model 2, $\int_{50}^{80}l(a)\,da = 1{,}602.0$ man-years, and the total man-years lived is 16,090.6. The true value probably lies somewhere between these estimates.

For the two models, the proportion of the living population within different age intervals has been tabulated in Table 3, columns 6 and 8. The cumulative proportion is tabulated in columns 7 and 9. Note that the age distribution of the living population is necessarily more youthful than the age distribution of burials.

The life expectancy of the population is estimated as

$$\mathring{e}(0) = \frac{15{,}556.6}{533} = 29.19 \text{ years} \qquad (3\text{-}20)$$

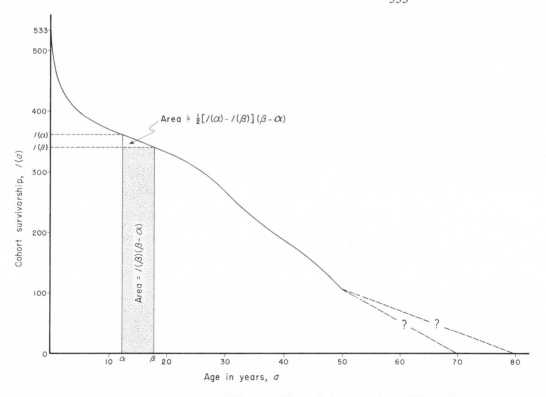

Figure 7. Survivorship curve for the Gibson-Klunk burial population, assuming stability and zero growth.

under Model 1. For those surviving to age 10, the expected lifespan is

$$10 + \mathring{e}(10) = 10 + \frac{\int_{10}^{\omega} l(a)\, da}{l(10)} = 40.70 \text{ years}$$

The crude birth rate b, estimated with Equation (3-13), is

$$b = \frac{1}{15,556.6/533}$$

$$= 0.0343 \text{ births/individual/year} \quad (3\text{-}21)$$

Because of the zero growth assumption, the crude death rate d must be equal to b.

For Model 2, the following statistics are obtained:

1. Life expectancy = $\mathring{e}(0)$ = 30.19 years.
2. Mean lifespan for survivors to age 10 = $\mathring{e}(10)$ = 42.13 years.
3. $b = d = 0.0331$.

When only the age distribution of deaths is known for a stable population with a given growth rate, further assumptions are required to calculate age-specific fertility rates. We know, however, that fertility must satisfy Equations (3-15) and (3-11), i.e.,

$$\int_u^v e^{-ra}p(a)m(a)\, da$$

$$= R' \int_u^v e^{-ra}p(a)F(a)\, da = 1 \quad (3\text{-}22)$$

and this is enough to establish some weak constraints on the value of the gross reproduction rate R'. The factor e^{-ra} is a constant equal to 1 in the stationary case. However, we retain it in the ensuing discussion so that the reasoning will apply to growing and declining populations as well.

Let G_{min} represent the minimum value of $e^{-ra}p(a)$ during the childbearing age and G_{max} its maximum value. Since $\int_u^v F(a)\, da = 1$, replacing $e^{-ra}p(a)$ with G_{min} in Equation (3-22) yields the inequality $G_{min} < 1/R'$. Replacing $e^{-ra}p(a)$ with G_{max} gives $G_{max} > 1/R'$. For $r \geqslant 0$, $G_{min} = e^{-ru}p(u)$ and $G_{max} = e^{-rv}p(v)$ since $e^{-ra}p(a)$ must then decrease monotonically with increasing age.

Now consider the stationary case specifically. Effectively, the age of childbearing lies between 15 and 45 years. Thus, R' is limited by the inequality

$$\frac{1}{p(15)} = 1.52 < R' < \frac{1}{p(45)} = 3.45$$

In Equations (3-15) and (3-11), the $p(a)$ values are female survival probabilities, but in these and subsequent computations it was assumed that probabilities established for the two-sex population are adequate approximations for females alone.

If one is willing to assume that a woman's age at death is not correlated with her previous fertility experience, then $2R'$ gives completed family size (both male and female children) for women who survive beyond the childbearing age. Lower and upper bounds for $2R'$ are 3.03 and 6.90 children.

In general, with survivorship given, Equation (3-22) requires smaller values for $R' = \int_u^v m(a)\, da$ if the set of age-specific fertility rates inclines toward younger childbearing ages, and larger values if fertility is greater during older ages. The maximum values of $m(a)$ are limited by biological factors which determine a minimum possible value for mean birth intervals in populations. The incidence of sterility, the interval between attempted and successful conception, the time lost by fetal deaths, the 9-month period of full-term pregnancy, and the duration of anovulatory cycles and lactational amenorrhea in the postpartum period, contribute to a *mean* minimum spacing of births of more than 16½ months (Wrigley 1969:92-94). Thus, solely for biological reasons, $m(a)$ at any age must have an expected value less than ½ × 12/16½ = 0.364 female births per woman per year. Wrigley remarks that populations practicing neither abortion nor contraception often have birth intervals from 35 to 50 months among women in their early twenties, the period of maximum fertility. By assigning all births to either extreme of the childbearing age, subject to biological restrictions on the maximum value of $m(a) = 0.364$, and solving Equation (3-22) for these extreme cases, we can calculate a marginally smaller range for R' of 1.55 to 2.92. For completed family size, the range is narrowed to between 3.10 and 5.84 offspring. With a careful enumeration of other biological constraints, the range could undoubtedly be restricted even more.

If assumptions are permitted about age-specific fertility based on experience with better documented populations, then much more fertility information can be extracted from a prehistoric burial population. *The Concept of a Stable Population* (United Nations 1968:39) states:

> The variation in the female fertility rate as a function of the age of the woman always follows the same pattern, beginning from zero at about 15 years of age, rising to a maximum between 20 and 30, and then declining until it returns to zero at about the age of 50.

This pattern reflects both biological and social

TABLE 4. *Ranges for Annual Age-Specific Female Fertility Rates* m(a) *in the Community that Produced the Gibson-Klunk Burial Population*

| Age a | Age distribution of fertility rates[a] $\int_a^{a+5} F(a)\,da$ | | Gibson-Klunk age-specific fertility rate $m(a)$, as fitted against the 2 models | | | |
| | | | Growth rate: $r = 0$ | | Growth rate: $r = 0.02$ | |
	Jamaican[b]	Spanish[b]	Jamaican	Spanish	Jamaican	Spanish
15	0.136	0.014	0.051	0.006	0.065	0.008
20	.292	.147	.109	.060	.139	.081
25	.249	.303	.093	.125	.119	.166
30	.166	.272	.062	.112	.079	.149
35	.110	.179	.041	.074	.052	.098
40	.047	.085	.018	.035	.022	.047

[a]In discrete notation, $_5F_a$.

[b]*Source*: United Nations (1968:40).

patterns in fertility. The publication notes that the age distribution of fertility $F(a)$ varies relatively little throughout the world in comparison with schedules of age-specific fertility rates $m(a)$: Among distributions recently observed in 52 countries (all the data are in the United Nations *Demographic Yearbook, 1954*), the extremes in the distribution of $F(a)$ were recorded in Jamaica, 1951, and in Spain, 1940. Fertility age distributions for these two countries are given in Table 4. Presumably, the true value of R' and most of all true values of $m(a)$ (at least those near the beginning and end of the childbearing period) for the Gibson-Klunk population will be intermediate to the results obtained by fitting the extreme Jamaican and Spanish distributions to the prehistoric burial data.

To obtain gross reproduction rates for Gibson-Klunk with the aid of these fertility distributions, it is necessary to solve a discrete analog for Equation (3-22). The age distributions of fertility for Jamaica and Spain are reported for 5-year intervals: $\int_a^{a+5} F(a)\,da$. Proceeding as if $m(a)$ were constant within these intervals, Equation (3-22) is approximated, with $r \geq 0$, as

$$\frac{1}{R'} \doteq \sum_{a=u}^{v-5} \left[\frac{e^{-ra}p(a) + e^{-r(a+5)}p(a+5)}{2} \right] {}_5F_a \quad (3\text{-}23)$$

(see United Nations 1968:40). Hence, the gross reproduction rate under the Jamaican extreme, with $r = 0$, is computed as

$$\frac{1}{R'_J} \doteq (0.643 \times 0.136) + (0.607 \times 0.292)$$

$$+ \ldots + (0.323 \times 0.047) = 0.535$$

i.e., $R'_J = 1.87$. Similarly, R'_S under the Spanish

extreme is 2.06. Completed family size (approximated by $2R'$) should then fall in the range of 3.74 to 4.11 children.

Since

$$m(a) = R'F(a) \doteq R' \left[\frac{\int_a^{a+5} F(x)\,dx}{5} \right] \quad (3\text{-}24)$$

for a in the interval $(a, a+5)$, a range for prehistoric female age-specific fertilities is easily obtained. Values for the Jamaican and Spanish extremes are presented in Table 4.

Discrete counterparts for integral notation

Let $_nL_a$ represent the number of man-years lived between ages a and $a + n$ in the cohort. This may be estimated as

$$_nL_a \doteq nl(a') \doteq \frac{n}{2}\left[l(a) + l(a + n) \right] \quad (3\text{-}19')$$

Using Equation (3-14'), the proportion $_nC_a$ of the (stationary) population within an age interval is

$$_nC_a \doteq \frac{n_a l(a')}{\sum_{x=0}^{\omega} n_x l(x')} \doteq \frac{_nL_a}{\sum_{x=0}^{\omega} {}_nL_x} \quad (3\text{-}18')$$

The values of $_nL_a$ are given in column 5 of Table 3. The percentage of the entire population that is less than age a is,

$$\sum_{x=0}^{a} {}_nC_x$$

Life expectancy is computed as

$$\mathring{e}(a) \doteq a + \frac{\sum_{x=a}^{\omega} {}_nL_x}{l(a)} \quad (3\text{-}20')$$

and the crude birth rate as

$$b \doteq \frac{1}{\Sigma_{a=0}^{\omega} {}_nL_a/l(0)} \qquad (3\text{-}21')$$

For the discussions of fertility, first note from Equations (3-10) and (3-11) that

$$m(a') \doteq \frac{R'_n F_a}{n_a} \qquad (3\text{-}24')$$

so that in discrete form, Equation (3-22) becomes

$$\sum_{a=u}^{v} n_a e^{-ra'} p(a') m(a')$$

$$\doteq \sum_{a=u}^{v} e^{-ra'} p(a') {}_nF_a R' \doteq 1 \qquad (3\text{-}22')$$

Case of a Stable, Growing Population ($r = 0.02$)

Relationship of age distribution of burials to cohort deaths

As in the case of $r = 0$, the age distribution of burials must be related to the life history of a cohort of arbitrary initial size. An intuitive discussion of the problem appears below, and a more rigorous approach appears in Appendix B, Statements 1 and 2.

Stability implies that the age distribution of deaths in a population is time-invariant; hence, the age distribution of a burial population also represents the mortality pattern in a community at any moment of time. Furthermore, if migration does not disturb the community age structure, the community can be studied as if it were closed to migration.

It is only necessary, then, to show how to transform the age distribution of deaths in a population during an arbitrary moment of time (t, $t + dt$) into a new distribution for the history of death of the cohort born during the same interval. Though cohorts in a stable, growing population are successively larger in size, only vital statistics of absolute size are affected.

The exponential growth formula for an entire population, Equation (3-12), applies equally to the growth of age classes. After a period of time s, all age classes in a population increase by the same factor e^{rs}, and because mortality probabilities have not changed, the number of deaths in each age class also increases by the factor e^{rs}. The cohort born at time t will be represented at time $t + a$ by the entire class of individuals who are a years old. So if at time t there are $d(a, t) \, da \, dt$ deaths observed among individuals of age a, then at time $t + a$ there must be

$$d(a, t + a) \, da \, dt = e^{ra} d(a, t) \, da \, dt$$

deaths among those of age a, i.e., among the survivors of the cohort born at time t.

This establishes the required relationship between cohort and burial population: The number of deaths between ages a and $a + da$ in a cohort is directly proportional to e^{ra} times the number of deaths between ages a and $a + da$ in the burial population. Or for age intervals of measurable width, for instance between a and β, it is *approximately* true that the number of deaths is directly proportional to $e^{r(a+\beta)/2}$ times the number of deaths within the corresponding age interval of the burial population (see Comments, Statement 2, App. B). For convenience, we fix the arbitrary, initial size of the cohort as the sum of a weighted number of deaths for each age class of the burial population, the weighting factor being $e^{r(a+\beta)/2}$. For example, 47.6 deaths are recorded for the Gibson-Klunk 45 to 50 year age class, and the arbitrary cohort correspondingly suffers a loss of $47.6 e^{0.02 \times 47.5} = 47.6 e^{0.95} = 123.1$ individuals during this 5-year interval. The number of deaths in each age interval for this arbitrary cohort is recorded in Table 5, column 2, and the relationship between the age structure of deaths in the cohort and in the burial population is displayed graphically in Figure 8. The arbitrary initial size of the cohort (the sum of column 2) is 1,048.7 individuals. (See Fig. 4 for comparisons of the age distribution of deaths in the burial population and in the cohorts resulting from assuming $r = 0$ and $r = 0.02$.)

For the over-50 group, the adjustment was made by using the Model 1 assumption introduced for the stationary case (i.e., $\omega = 70$) and multiplying the observed death rate by $e^{0.02 \times [50+70]/2}$.

Note that for a growing population we were obliged to make an approximation for the distribution of mortality among old adults *before* a survivorship curve could be calculated, whereas in the stationary case survivorship below age 50 required no assumption about the subsequent pattern of mortality.

Vital statistics for Gibson-Klunk ($r = 0.02$)

The procedure for calculating survivorship and age-specific mortality rates is similar to that for the stationary case. These life table statistics are presented in Table 5, columns 3, 4, and 9. Calculation of the age structure for the living population must consider that older age groups come from smaller initial cohorts in a growing

TABLE 5. *Life Table for the Gibson-Klunk Burial Population, Assuming Stability and a Two Percent Annual Growth Rate* (r = 0.02)

(1) Age in years a	(2) Number of deaths for hypothetical cohort $\int_a^{a+n} e^{ra}D(a)\,da$	(3) Survivorship $l(a)$	(4) Survival probability $p(a)$	(5) Man-years lived during age interval $(a,a+n)$ by all of hypothetical cohort $\int_a^{a+n} l(a)\,da$	(6) $\int_a^{a+n} e^{-ra}l(a)\,da$	(7) Proportion of living pop. within age interval $(a,a+n)$ $\int_a^{a+n} c(a)\,da$	(8) Proportion of living pop. less than age a $\int_a^a c(a)\,da$	(9) Annual mortality rate $n\bar{\mu}_a$	(10) Age in years a
0	63.2	1,048.7	1	1,017.1	1,007.0	.177	0	.0622	0
1	36.2	985.5	.940	967.4	938.8	⎱	.039	.0208	1
2	22.8	949.3	.905	937.9	892.2	⎰	.076	⎰	2
3	19.8	926.5	.884	1,833.2	1,692.3	.150	.111	.0058	3
5	26.0	906.7	.865	4,468.5	3,846.1	.132	.177	.0063	5
10	27.1	880.7	.840	4,335.8	3,376.7	.132	.327	.0063	10
15	25.1	853.6	.814	4,205.2	2,963.4	.116	.458	.0060	15
20	33.9	828.5	.790	4,057.8	2,587.4	.186	.574	.0084	20
25	78.3	794.6	.758	3,777.2	2,179.3	.124	.675	.0207	25
30	79.7	716.3	.683	3,382.3	1,765.7	.124	.760	.0236	30
35	74.7	636.6	.607	2,996.2	1,415.3	.075	.828	.0250	35
40	84.2	561.9	.536	2,599.0	1,110.9	.075	.884	.0325	40
45	123.1	477.7	.456	2,080.8	804.7	.075	.927	.0596	45
50	354.6	354.6	.338	3,546.0	1,068.0	.042	.958	—	50
ω	—	0	0	—	—	.042	1	—	ω
	Σ = 1048.7			Σ = 40,204.4					

Note: In discrete notation (see App. A), columns 2, 5, 6, 7, and 8 are, respectively, $e^{ra'}{}_nD_a$, $_nL_a$, $e^{-ra'}{}_nL_a$, $_nC_a$, and $\sum_{x=0}^{a}{}_nC_x$ (where $a' = a + \tfrac{1}{2}n$).

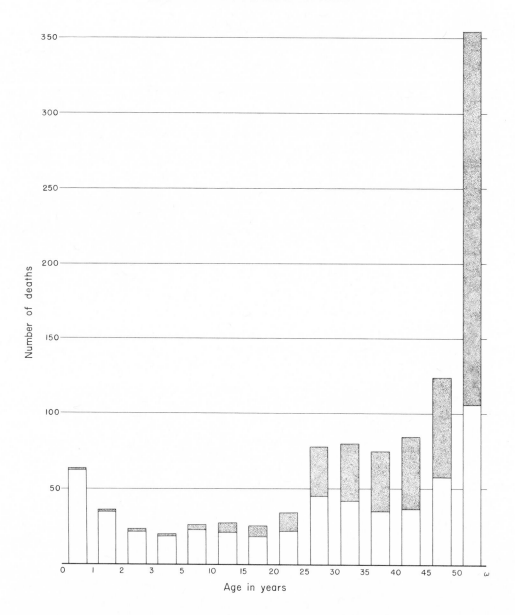

Figure 8. Generation of the age structure of death for a cohort from the age distribution of the Gibson-Klunk burial population, assuming an annual growth rate of 2 percent. Height of unshaded portion of bars indicates number of individuals of specified age in the burial population; total height of bars indicates number of deaths in the hypothetical cohort, obtained by application of the exponential adjustment factor exp[0.02 (a + β)/2]. Maximal age ω is assumed to be 70 years.

population. Thus, instead of having

$$c(a)\,da = \frac{l(a)\,da}{\int_0^\omega l(x)\,dx}$$

as in the stationary case,

$$c(a)\,da = \frac{e^{-ra}l(a)\,da}{\int_0^\omega e^{-rx}l(x)\,dx} \qquad (3\text{-}25)$$

is the appropriate formula. This increases the size of younger age classes relative to older ones, providing a more youthful population profile. For example, assuming $r = 0.02$, the median age for the community is 17 years; whereas with $r = 0$, it is 20. Results of age structure computations are given in columns 6, 7, and 8 of Table 5.

In a growing population, life expectancy is not

identical to the mean age of death in the mortuary population. The hypothetical cohort of 1048.7 individuals live a total of 40,204.4 man-years, giving an estimated life expectancy of $\overset{\circ}{e}(0)$ = 40,204.4/1,048.7 = 38.34 years, as opposed to a mean age at death in the burial population of 29.19 years. For those surviving to age 10, the mean lifespan is $10 + \overset{\circ}{e}(10) = 10 + (30,980.3/880.7) = 45.18$ years. The crude birth rate is

$$\frac{1}{\int_0^\omega e^{-ra}l(a)\,da/l(0)} = \frac{1}{25,647.8/1048.7} = 0.0409$$

births per person per year; and since $d = b - r$, the crude death rate is 0.0209.

Because of the constraints on fertility rates represented by Equation (3-22), the gross reproduction rate is limited by

$$\frac{1}{e^{-15r}p(15)} < R' < \frac{1}{e^{-45r}p(45)}$$

thus, for $r = 0.02$,

$$1.66 < R' < 5.40$$

and the approximate completed family size lies within the range

$$3.32 < 2R' < 10.80$$

These limits are much too broad to be useful.

When a minimum spacing of 16½ months between births is added as a condition on fertility in Equation (3-22), the maximum bound for $2R'$ declines dramatically to 8.00; the lower bound is only marginally higher at 3.52. Careful consideration of biological restrictions on fertility, particularly as they are a function of age, should produce further substantial refinement of the range for R'.

Much more fertility information can be extracted from the Gibson-Klunk data if the less rigorous approach of reasoning from the fertility records of other populations is followed. Applying the extreme age distributions of fertility for Jamaica, 1951, and Spain, 1940, to the Gibson-Klunk situation results in limits of $R'_J = 2.38$ and $R'_S = 2.75$ for the gross reproduction rate, with an approximate range of 4.76 to 5.49 children of both sexes for completed family size.

Calculations of $m(a)$ for the two cases, using Equation (3-24), are presented in Table 4, columns 6 and 7. At least for ages near the lower and upper ends of the childbearing period, the true values of $m(a)$ (assuming $r = 0.02$) should lie between the corresponding values for the two countries.

Discrete counterparts for integral notation

To compute age structure, use

$$nC_a \doteq \frac{n_a e^{-ra'}l(a')}{\Sigma_{x=0}^\omega n_x e^{-rx'}l(x')} \doteq \frac{e^{-ra'}{}_nL_a}{\Sigma_{x=0}^\omega e^{-rx'}{}_nL_x} \quad (3\text{-}25')$$

Life expectancy and birth rate are calculated by the same formulae as for the stationary case, except that the weighting factors $e^{-ra'}$ must be included in the same manner as in the above age structure computation.

3. EVALUATION OF VITAL STATISTICS

Having completed the life table computations, some important interpretative questions remain: (1) Are some age classes of the Gibson-Klunk burial population underrepresented? (2) Can a value for r be chosen and defended? (3) What consequences will the uncertainties of demographic reconstruction have for a regional population estimate? The estimated vital statistics will be examined for the evidence they provide concerning these questions.

Biased Representation of Age Classes

Assuming stability, the age structure of the living population is completely determined by mortality and fertility rates. One of the constraints imposed by stability, when $r \geqslant 0$, is that the proportion of the population within age intervals of equal width declines monotonically with increasing age. Under these conditions, an age distribution observed in *any* burial population will yield an age pyramid for the corresponding living population that is broadest for the newborn and narrows continuously to an apex at the oldest age. Thus, even when the stability assumption is untenable or when underrepresentation of some ages is pronounced, the estimated age structure for the living population is forced into a pyramid shape and may therefore seem reasonable.

The percentage distribution obtained for wide age intervals, such as for juveniles and adults, may have limited utility. Under the assumptions of $r = 0$ and $r = 0.02$, we find that 38.1 and 45.8 percent, respectively, of the living population that produced the Gibson-Klunk burials were less than 15 years old. Percentages in this range have been recorded by the censuses of several nonindustrial countries taken since the beginning of the twentieth century (United Nations 1956). Information about fertility and mortality rates is required to further interpret these percentages.

Crude birth and death rates are not informative. Neither rate reflects fertility or mortality alone, and their wide use in demography is largely due to the ease with which they can be calculated for living populations—even without knowledge of the population age structure. But, instead of being one step removed from the raw data on births and deaths, the crude rates for prehistoric populations lie at the end of a long chain of computations. The Gibson-Klunk birth and death rates are largely determined by the assumed value of r, since $r = b - d$.

Extreme estimates of the age-specific fertility rates $m(a)$ are as likely to result from the necessary assumptions about $F(a)$ as from any distortions caused by underrepresentation. The data on completed family size for women surviving the childbearing period are potentially more useful because of the convergence obtained when the extreme Jamaican and Spanish fertility distributions were fitted to the Gibson-Klunk survivorship information. For $r = 0$, we estimated between 3.74 and 4.11 births for women who survived to age 45; for $r = 0.02$, between 4.76 and 5.49 births per woman. Nag (1962:169-171) has compiled statistics of the average number of live births for women past childbearing age in 46 non-European societies. Ten of these had smaller values than the lower limit of 3.74 calculated for Gibson-Klunk with $r = 0$; 22 had values greater than the upper value of 5.49 children calculated for Gibson-Klunk with $r = 0.02$. The range in these societies was from 2.6 to 10.4 children. Though he does not discuss specific cases, Nag himself (1962:16) has questioned the accuracy of the sources. One suspects the statistics tend to underestimate the true number. Seldom will too many children be attributed to a woman, but infant deaths are generally regarded to be underreported in censuses. Possibly a range of 3.74 to 4.11 children per woman at Gibson-Klunk is low, but the case is inherently weak because of the potential for cultural control of fertility.

The best indicators of bias in a burial population are the estimated age-specific mortality rates (Caughley 1966). Buikstra (1972) compared the rates for Gibson-Klunk with a series of mortality tables published by the United Nations (1955). The U.N. tables do not describe actual populations, but are models typifying mortality patterns from birth to age 85 under a series of different life expectancies. The models are based on a worldwide sample of 158 twentieth century censuses from 50 nations. They are generated from this sample by calculating parabolic regressions between the mortality rates observed for adjacent age groups and by starting each model for a different arbitrary value of infant mortality.

Eighteen of the census populations had life expectancies of less than 40 years: Only three of the censuses (all for India) reported life expectancies of less than 30 years; eight reported life expectancies of 30 to 35 years, and seven, below 40 years. Particularly for life expectancies below 30 years, the models are suspect because of the small sample of high-mortality populations. Also, they are intended only to provide a single typical mortality curve for a given life expectancy, and the significance of deviations from the model in real populations is not considered.

Nevertheless, Buikstra concluded that a reasonable correspondence existed between the Gibson-Klunk series and one of the models. Certainly the U-shaped curve of age-specific mortality rates for the mound population, expected on theoretical grounds, is important evidence for a reasonably good representation of all age classes. However, a case can still be made for considerable deviation of the Gibson-Klunk mortality rates from the U.N. series of models. The largest deviations occur for the age groups subject to highest mortality. The standard models were plotted on a logarithmic scale (United Nations 1955:22), thus deemphasizing differences at the higher levels of mortality. Consequently, on this scale, a comparison of the standard models with the Gibson-Klunk mortality rates minimizes the apparent differences.

Rates are replotted in Figure 9 for some of the models and for the Gibson-Klunk populations, without employing the logarithmic transformation, and following the U.N. publication in reporting mortality rates not as $_n\bar{\mu}_a$, but rather as $_nq_a$, defined as

$$_nq_a = \frac{l(a) - l(a + n)}{l(a)}$$

That is, if a cohort has $l(a)$ surviving members at age a, then the fraction of these survivors who die before age $a + n$ is $_nq_a$. Except for $_1q_0$ and $_4q_1$, all mortality rates in the figure are calculated for 5-year intervals. The curves indicate considerable deviation for the first year of life and between the ages of 25 and 50, i.e., for the groups with higher mortality.

In Figure 10, Gibson-Klunk age-specific mortality rates are compared with the distribution of mortality rates in the 18 populations of the U.N. sample having life expectancies of less than 40

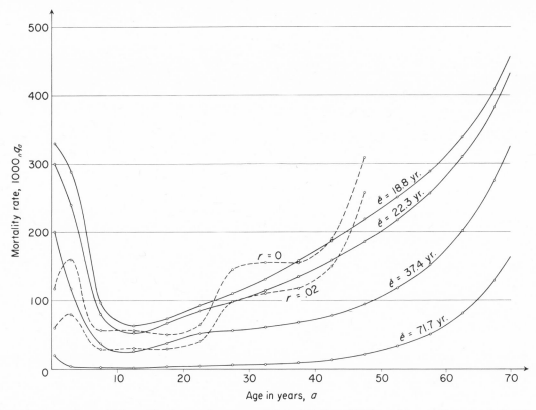

Figure 9. Comparison of Gibson-Klunk mortality rates and United Nations (1955) model mortality rates. Broken lines indicate Gibson-Klunk rate. Curves were plotted using $_1q_0$, $_4q_1$, and, for older age groups, $_5q_a$.

years. Both the stationary and the 2 percent growth models for Gibson-Klunk give values of $_1q_0$ that are smaller than for any of the 18 census populations. Though the deviation of the zero-growth model is less extreme, allowance must be made for the fact that 15 of the 18 comparative populations had higher life expectancies than the Gibson-Klunk population under the zero-growth model. In fact, every one of the 46 nations in the U.N. sample with life expectancies of less than 50 years had higher mortality rates during the first year of life than did the Gibson-Klunk population. The value of $_4q_1$ is lower for the 2 percent growth model than for any of the 18 census populations, but the zero-growth model for this interval fits well within the range of the U.N. sample. As expected theoretically, the age-specific mortality clearly declines between ages 0 and 5 for both the zero-growth and 2 percent growth reconstructions. Nevertheless this comparison still strongly suggests that infants are underrepresented.

Missing infants seriously affect some paleodemographic statistics. One statistic strongly affected by their absence is the computed life

expectancy. To illustrate, suppose the true infant mortality rate for the community associated with the Gibson-Klunk mounds was $_1\bar{\mu}_0$ = 0.250 in the first year of life rather than the computed value of 0.125 for zero growth; i.e., half of the infants do not appear in the burial population. True life expectancy then would be reduced from the estimated 29.19 years (Model 1: ω = 70) to 25.8 years.

Fortunately, the effect of missing infants on the variable of man-years is minimal. Suppose these infants in the illustration above each lived for one-half year. Their contribution to the true value for man-years would raise the total imperceptibly to 15,592.1 man-years from the level of 15,556.6 man-years computed from the mound burial population alone.

Another marked discrepancy between mortality in the Gibson-Klunk population and the 18 censuses occurs for older age groups (Fig. 10). From ages 25 to 50—the last age for which computations can be made—mortality rates for Gibson-Klunk under the zero-growth assumption are higher than any of the 18 census populations. For 2 percent

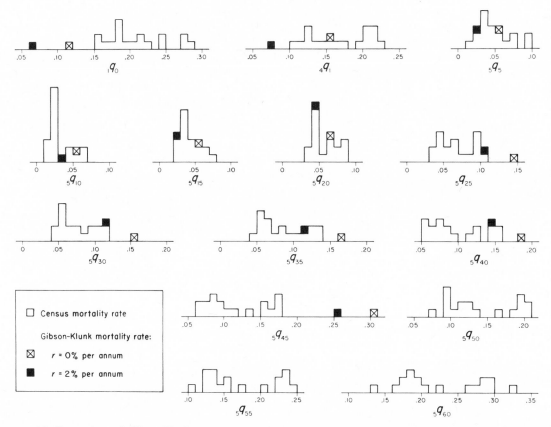

Figure 10. Comparison of Gibson-Klunk mortality rates with mortality rates from 18 twentieth century populations having life expectancies of less than 40 years. Data for the 18 censuses are from United Nations (1955).

growth, higher mortality is estimated only for the age class of 45 to 50 years.

Underrepresentation in a mound population which *elevates* reconstructed mortality rates above the true values is an indication of serious problems for population estimation. Since mortality rates for a specified age interval $(a, a + n)$ are calculated by the formula

$$ {}_n\bar{\mu}_a = \frac{\ln l(a) - \ln l(a + n)}{n} $$

the mortality rate can be too large only if $l(a + n)$ is too small; this can result only from underrepresentation of individuals *older* than age $a + n$. Since older skeletons in a burial population contribute proportionately more to the statistic of total man-years than the younger ones, their absence leads to far greater bias in a population estimate.

Underrepresentation of the elderly is not conclusive, however. Three other Illinois burial populations (or samples thereof), including two far removed in time from the Middle Woodland period, present adult mortality curves as extreme

as those obtained for the Gibson-Klunk Middle Woodland population (Table 6). These include the Archaic component of the Pete Klunk mound group, the Dickson mound Middle Mississippi population (both reported in Blakely 1971), and the Albany mound group series of Middle Woodland skeletons (Jamison 1971). It is possible that similar mortuary practices were responsible for underrepresentation of older adults in each case. However, in many other respects, the mortuary customs of these populations are distinctive, and in view of the large timespan represented by the three cases, the prior probability of similar treatment of the elderly does not seem high.

More burial populations should be examined— from the Midwest, from the New World, and from pre-twentieth century populations in general— before firm conclusions about the causes of high adult mortality estimates can be drawn. However, this phenomenon appears to be characteristic of a large percentage of early burial populations. For instance, assuming zero growth, the Indian Knoll, Kentucky, series of Archaic skeletons (Johnston

TABLE 6. *Comparison of Annual Adult Mortality Rates $_n\bar{\mu}_a$ for Three Illinois Burial Populations*

Age	Gibson-Klunk (Middle Woodland)[a]		Klunk (Archaic)[b] $r = 0$	Dickson mounds (Middle Mississippi)[b] $r = 0$	Albany mounds (Middle Woodland)[c] $r = 0$
	$r = 0$	$r = 0.02$			
20-25	0.0134	0.0084	} 0.0187	} 0.0329	} 0.0832
25-30	.0312	.0207			
30-35	.0338	.0236	.0391	} .0511	
35-40	.0340	.0250			
40-45	.0419	.0325	} .0738	} .0952	
45-50	.0737	.0596			

[a]Calculated from age distribution data provided by Jane E. Buikstra.
[b]Calculated from age distribution in Blakely (1971); annual mortality rate is for 10-year age intervals.
[c]Calculated from age distribution data in Jamison (1971); annual mortality rate is for age class of 21 to 35 years.

and Snow 1961; Snow 1948) gives mortality rates $_5\bar{\mu}_a$ of 0.0357, 0.0543, 0.0984, and 0.2790 per year for the four 5-year age classes between 20 and 40 years. These rates are uniformly higher than the corresponding values calculated for the Gibson-Klunk Middle Woodland skeletons. Going farther afield, mortality rates calculated for Pecos Pueblo (Kidder 1958) are 0.0106 for a 20 to 30 year age class, but 0.0813 for the 30 to 50 year class. Data on skeletal populations compiled by Vallois (1960) and by Brothwell (1972), primarily for pre-modern European populations, disclose numerous additional cases of adult mortality rates on the order of those calculated for Gibson-Klunk.* In this study, I have assumed, therefore, that older adults are correctly represented among the Gibson-Klunk burials.

Choosing a Value for Growth Rate

Population estimates based on burial populations vary with the choice of a growth rate r because of the effects of r on the intermediate variable of *number of man-years* represented by a burial population. This definition of the intermediate variable is ambiguous, and two meanings should be distinguished. Let the time period under investigation have the initial date $t = 0$ and terminal date $t = s$. One meaning is "the cumulative number of years lived by all persons who died between $t = 0$ and $t = s$." This number is, of course, directly measurable as the sum of ages of all individuals dying during that time interval, and it is represented symbolically as

$$s\bar{A} = \int_0^\omega \int_0^s ad(a, t)\, dt\, da$$

$$= \int_0^\omega \int_0^s ak(a,t)\mu(a)\, dt\, da \qquad (3\text{-}26)$$

*See also data in K. Weiss (1973), published since the completion of this manuscript.

where $\bar{A}$ is the mean age of the burial population. The second meaning is "the total number of years lived by the prehistoric population between $t = 0$ and $t = s$," and it is represented as

$$s\bar{K} = \int_0^\omega \int_0^s k(a, t)\, dt\, da \qquad (3\text{-}27)$$

where $\bar{K}$ is the mean age of the living population during the period. Lacking information about the *date* of burial of members of the mortuary population, one can infer the value of this variable only by making certain restrictive demographic assumptions (Caughley 1966).

In order to relate these definitions numerically, observe that the $k(a, 0)\, da$ persons who are of age a at time $t = 0$ have lived a cumulative total of $ak(a, 0)\, da$ man-years; thus the entire population alive at that time has lived

$$\bar{C}(0)K(0) = \int_0^\omega ak(a, 0)\, da \qquad (3\text{-}28)$$

man-years, where $\bar{C}(0)$ is the mean age of the living population at $t = 0$. These man-years are *included* under the first definition. Similarly, the population alive at time $t = s$ has lived

$$\bar{C}(s)K(s) = \int_0^\omega ak(a, s)\, da \qquad (3\text{-}29)$$

man-years. This quantity is *excluded* under the first definition. Therefore, the burial population accumulated during time interval $(0, s)$ has lived

$$s\bar{A} = \bar{C}(0)K(0) + s\bar{K} - \bar{C}(s)K(s)$$

$$= \int_0^\omega \int_0^s ad(a, t)\, dt\, da$$

$$= \int_0^\omega ak(a, 0)\, da$$

$$+ \int_0^\omega \int_0^s k(a, t)\, dt\, da - \int_0^\omega ak(a, s)\, da \qquad (3\text{-}30)$$

man-years. If the first and third terms are equal in value, the two definitions of man-years, expressed by Equations (3-27) and (3-30), converge. This would be the case if the size of each age class at $t =$

s were the same as at $t = 0$. The two definitions will be nearly equivalent—even in a population having an instable age structure—provided that the total population size is approximately the same at $t = 0$ and $t = s$ or provided that the second term of Equation (3-30) is large in proportion to the difference of the first and third terms. The greatest percentage divergence will arise between the alternate definitions under a high rate of population growth or decline, which makes the difference between $\bar{C}(0)K(0) = \int_0^\omega ak(a, 0)\,da$ and $\bar{C}(s)K(s) = \int_0^\omega ak(a, s)\,da$ large in proportion to the middle term of Equation (3-30). Manipulation of these identities will show that for stable populations the percentage divergence is a function of the growth rate r and the mortality structure $p(a)$, but not of the duration s of the time period. Specifically, the ratio of Equation (3-30) to Equation (3-27) has the value

$$1 - r\left[\frac{\int_0^\omega ae^{-ra}p(a)\,da}{\int_0^\omega e^{-ra}p(a)\,da}\right] = 1 - r\bar{C}$$

where $\bar{C}$ is the mean age of the living population.

For stable, stationary populations, the distinction in definitions of man-years is trivial because both then have identical numerical values (neglecting minor deviations of mortality and fertility rates from the corresponding probabilities). In fact, all of the following quantities are equal in stable, stationary populations:

1. $D\bar{A}$ = total man-years lived by a burial population.
2. $D\overset{\circ}{e}(0)$.
3. D/d = total man-years lived by the community contemporary with the accumulating burial population.
4. $l(0)\overset{\circ}{e}(0)$ = total man-years lived by the arbitrary cohort used in estimating vital statistics.

D = total size of the burial population and

$$\bar{A} = \frac{\int_0^\omega aD(a)\,da}{D} \tag{3-31}$$

is the mean age at death in the burial population.

Quantities (2) and (4) are equal because $D = l(0)$ by definition. Quantities (1), (2), and (3) must be equal if $\bar{A} = \overset{\circ}{e}(0) = 1/d$. To show that $\overset{\circ}{e}(0) = 1/d$, use Equations (3-9) and (3-13):

$$\overset{\circ}{e}(0) = \frac{\int_0^\omega l(a)\,da}{l(0)}$$

$$= \int_0^\omega p(a)\,da = \frac{1}{b} = \frac{1}{d} \tag{3-32}$$

To show that $\bar{A} = \overset{\circ}{e}(0)$ in a stationary population, note that $D(a)\,da = l(a)\mu(a)\,da$; hence,

$$\bar{A} = \frac{\int_0^\omega aD(a)\,da}{D} = \frac{\int_0^\omega al(a)\mu(a)\,da}{l(0)}$$

But from the definition of $\mu(a)$ in Equation (3-5), we know that

$$l(a)\mu(a) = -\frac{dl(a)}{da}$$

Integrating by parts gives

$$\int_0^\omega al(a)\mu(a)\,da = [-al(a)] \Big|_0^\omega - [-\int_0^\omega l(a)\,da]$$

$$= 0 + \int_0^\omega l(a)\,da \tag{3-33}$$

Thus,

$$\bar{A} = \frac{\int_0^\omega l(a)\,da}{l(0)} = \overset{\circ}{e}(0) \tag{3-34}$$

(see proof in Keyfitz 1968:6).

For $r \neq 0$ in a stable population, none of the four statistics listed above are equivalent. The value of $D\bar{A}$ remains the same for all values of r. For Gibson-Klunk, it was $533 \times 29.19 = 15,556.6$ man-years. If $r = 0.02$, $D\overset{\circ}{e}(0) = 20,433.0$ man-years,

$$D/d = \int_0^\omega e^{-ra}l(a)\,da = 25,646.6 \text{ man-years} \tag{3-35}$$

and $l(0)\overset{\circ}{e}(0) = 1048.7 \times 38.34 = 40,202.8$ man-years. $D\overset{\circ}{e}(0)$ and $l(0)\overset{\circ}{e}(0)$ describe neither the burial population nor its contemporary community. That D/d and $\int_0^\omega e^{-ra}l(a)\,da$ should be equal and that they should represent the number of man-years lived by the community contemporary with the accumulating burial population is not immediately obvious, and proof is provided in Appendix B, Statements 3 and 4. The value obtained for D/d is 64.9 percent larger than the number of years (15,556.6) lived by the individuals that were actually interred at the burial site.

The number of man-years lived by the prehistoric populations contemporary with the accumulating burial population (i.e., the second definition of man-years) is the correct statistic to use in estimating population size.

A dilemma is posed therefore by the dependence of the statistic on the value chosen for r, since the age distribution of burials and resulting demographic reconstructions give few clues about the true value of the growth rate.

Carrier (1958) provides a method for computing r based on a comparison of the prehistoric mortality data against the U.N. model life tables.

We shall not employ it, however, for the following reasons:

1. The sample used to construct the model life tables is very small for populations having life expectancies less than 40 years.
2. Use of the method makes no allowance for the deviation of empirically obtained life tables from the family of model life tables.

In short, this method of constraining the value of r involves additional dubious assumptions.

Another approach to the problem suggests that man-years computed from the regional Middle Woodland period burial population will be close to the number of man-years lived in the region during the Middle Woodland period. This claim rests on the case for a narrow range of near-zero values for r.

Consider growth at a continuously compounding mean rate of 2 percent per year for the 550 years of the Middle Woodland period. From Equation (3-12),

$$K(550) = e^{0.02 \times 550} K(0) = 59,874 K(0)$$

Thus, an initial population of 100 would grow to almost 6,000,000 after 550 years. Obviously, a growth rate of this magnitude maintained over the entire Middle Woodland period is impossible. In fact, an annual growth rate of just 0.42 percent maintained over 550 years will increase a population tenfold, and growth of 0.84 percent will give a hundredfold increase. A tenfold increase of the lower Illinois Valley Middle Woodland population must be regarded as a maximal estimate of growth given present knowledge of the relative size, abundance, and intensity of occupation of Early, Middle, and Late Woodland sites. Thus, a growth rate of between 0 and 0.42 percent per year is a reasonable range for the *mean* Middle Woodland value of r. Applying the maximum of $r = 0.0042$ to the Gibson-Klunk burial population results in an increase of 1.99 years in life expectancy over the stationary model—to 31.18 years. The total man-years lived by the contemporary community increases from 15,556.6 to 17,171.7 years (an increase of 10.4 percent). Relative to other uncertainties in a regional population estimate, the assumption of zero growth is a minor distortion.

One problem remains: Though the mean value of r for lower Illinois Valley Middle Woodland populations surely lies between 0 and 0.42 percent, any community, for a number of years,

could have grown more rapidly than this. Pooling the results from several mound groups in future estimates will minimize the effects of deviations from the mean value of r.

Discrete Counterparts for Integral Notation

For stable, stationary populations, mean age at death $\bar{A}$ in the burial population is

$$\bar{A} \doteq \frac{\Sigma_{a=0}^{\omega} a' {}_n D_a}{D} \qquad (3\text{-}31')$$

To show that $\mathring{e}(0) = 1/d$, use Equations (3-9′) and (3-13′):

$$\mathring{e}(0) = \frac{\Sigma_{a=0}^{\omega} n l(a')}{l(0)} = \sum_{a=0}^{\omega} n p(a')$$

$$= \sum_{a=0}^{\omega} e^{0 \cdot a'} n p(a') = \frac{1}{b} = \frac{1}{d} \qquad (3\text{-}32')$$

To show that $\bar{A} = \mathring{e}(0)$, assume for convenience that age intervals n have equal width. By definition,

$${}_n D_a = l(a) - l(a + n)$$

Hence,

$$\sum_{a=0}^{\omega} a' {}_n D_a \doteq \sum_{a=0}^{\omega} (a + \tfrac{1}{2} n) \, [l(a) - l(a + n)]$$

$$= \frac{n}{2} [l(0) - l(n)] + \frac{3n}{2} [l(n) - l(2n)] + \dots$$

$$+ \frac{(2\omega - 1)n}{2} [l(\omega - 1) - l(\omega)]$$

$$= \frac{n}{2} [l(0) + l(n)] + \frac{n}{2} [l(n) + l(2n)] + \dots$$

$$+ \frac{n}{2} [l(\omega - 2) - l(\omega - 1)] - \omega l(\omega)$$

$$\doteq \sum_{a=0}^{\omega} n l(a') \qquad (3\text{-}33')$$

where $l(a')$ is defined by Equation (3-19′). Since $D = l(0)$,

$$\bar{A} = \frac{\Sigma_{a=0}^{\omega} a' {}_n D_a}{D} = \frac{\Sigma_{a=0}^{\omega} n l(a')}{l(0)} = \mathring{e}(0) \quad (3\text{-}34')$$

as required.

For stable, growing populations,

$$\frac{D}{d} \doteq \sum_{a=0}^{\omega} n e^{-ra'} l(a') = \sum_{a=0}^{\omega} e^{-ra'} {}_n L_a \quad (3\text{-}35')$$

represents the number of man-years lived by the community contemporary with the accumulating burial population. Proof of this assertion will not be given for the discrete case, though it is developed for the continuous case in Appendix B.

4. SUMMARY

The Gibson-Klunk burial population was investigated with reference to three problems: (1) to determine man-years or mean age at death for use in population estimation; (2) to test for biased representation of age-sex classes, which might lead to unreliable population estimates; and (3) to show how several vital statistics may be calculated from the age-sex structure of a burial population.

First, there was the necessity for a general model that interrelates vital statistics. Only by making restrictive assumptions in the model was it possible to obtain vital statistics from a burial population that lacked exact information about dates of interment. The most important of the assumptions were (1) a stable age structure, (2) a specific value for rate of population growth r, and (3) a migration pattern that does not alter the age structure. Next, it was shown that for stationary populations, the resulting burial population can be considered as the remains of a single cohort. With adjustments for the effects of population growth, any stable population may be studied in the same way.

Values of $r = 0$ and $r = 0.02$ percent per year were chosen for illustrative purposes, and two sets of vital statistics were constructed for the Gibson-Klunk population. Among them were survival probabilities, age-specific mortality rates, life expectancy, crude death rate, crude birth rate, fertility rate, number of children born per woman completing reproductive lifespan, and age-structure of the prehistoric population.

Two statistics were useful in evaluating evidence for incomplete recovery of the community mortuary population: sex ratio and age-specific mortality rates. The former was near unity in the Gibson-Klunk population. Age-specific mortality rates were compared with the range of values obtained for twentieth century populations with high mortality, and this suggested that some infants were missing from the Gibson-Klunk burial population. However, because of their minor contribution to total man-years, missing infants will not seriously affect a population estimate. The proportion of older adults at Gibson-Klunk was also low by comparison with the twentieth century populations. However, high adult mortality rates have also been observed in a large percentage of other pre-Modern populations, thus suggesting that a problem of underrepresentation at Gibson-Klunk is not involved.

Choice of a value for r strongly affects estimates of the number of man-years lived during the time the burial population accumulated. However, it was shown that in the long run the mean value of r must be nearly zero.

4

The Population Estimates

In this chapter the population estimates are derived using data on the frequency and characteristics of Middle Woodland mound groups and villages in conjunction with demographic data from the preceding chapter. Emphasis is given to questions of completeness and reliability in the data base.

First, the Mound Survey method is employed to arrive at reasonable lower and upper bounds for the regional population level. Next the Mound-Village Calibration method provides another maximum estimate. Last is a discussion of ways of testing and refining the estimates in future investigations.

1. THE MOUND SURVEY METHOD

Procedure

We have found that D/d gives the total number of man-years lived during a time period of length L, where D is the number of individuals who died during the period and d is the crude death rate. (See "Choosing a Value for Growth Rate" in Sect. 3 of Chap. 3.) Consequently, mean population size P can be calculated as:

$$P = \frac{D}{Ld} \qquad (4\text{-}1)$$

This equation is the basis for the most direct estimate of population size for the lower Illinois Valley during the Middle Woodland period—the Mound Survey method.

For stable and stationary populations, the mean age at death $\bar{A}$ in the mortuary population is the reciprocal of the crude death rate:*

$$\bar{A} = \frac{1}{d}$$

However, $\bar{A}$ is less than $1/d$ for stable, growing populations and greater than $1/d$ for stable,

declining populations. The magnitude of the difference $1/d - \bar{A}$ depends on the value of the growth rate r, becoming greater as the absolute value of r increases. The growth rate is a statistic that cannot be estimated from the age distribution of a burial population. However, for the lower Illinois Valley Middle Woodland population, r probably had a value within the range of 0 and 0.42 percent per year (see Chap. 3, Sect. 3). If this is true, $1/d$ could exceed $\bar{A}$ by no more than 10 percent; $\bar{A}$ thus serves as a relatively good estimator of $1/d$. Because local values of the growth rate may vary over a considerably wider range than the regional value, the use of an estimate for $\bar{A}$ based upon a single burial population—the Gibson-Klunk series—is a major weakness of the study. But as age structures for more mound groups are determined, the pooled value for r should approach the regional value.

The Mound Survey method proposes that the total number of Middle Woodland individuals may be estimated from

$$D \doteq M\bar{N} \qquad (4\text{-}2)$$

where M is the number of Middle Woodland mound groups in the region and $\bar{N}$ is the mean size of a mound group burial population. Because mound destruction or interments in unmounded contexts may cause serious underestimation of D, the validity of Equation (4-2) must be assessed carefully. If its use is justified, then population size can be computed as

$$P \doteq \frac{M\bar{N}\bar{A}}{L} \qquad (4\text{-}3)$$

Values of $\bar{A}$ = 29.19 years (based on the Gibson-Klunk skeletal series) and of L = 550 years will be used in my estimates.

Distribution and Preservation of the Burials

Age-sex biases

A critical assumption underlying exact or maximum estimates is that most Middle Woodland

---

*This relationship also holds for a population which fluctuates because of migration, provided that the age structure of the population remains stable.

individuals received mound burial. Minimum estimates are also more refined if this practice was nearly universal. One test of the assumption is to examine the age-sex structure of mound populations for biases suggesting that unmounded burial or destruction of skeletons have been quantitatively important. Except for underrepresentation of infants, the age-sex structure of the Gibson-Klunk burials show no strong signs of bias as discussed in Chapter 3, Section 2. Even though the variables D and $\bar{A}$ *are* sensitive to undercounting in this age category, missing infants will not seriously affect population estimates because of their disproportionately small contribution to the total number of man-years lived by the population. Though D and $\bar{A}$ are, respectively, reduced and elevated above their true values, the deviations largely cancel each other in their product, i.e., in the estimate of man-years.

The mound population can provide no evidence for alternative mortuary practices if inclusion or exclusion of individuals from this population was independent of age and sex. Consequently, a direct search is required for unmounded Middle Woodland burials. But even if unmounded burials constitute a large proportion of the mortuary population, an estimate can be undertaken provided that these burials can be located systematically. The task would be rendered much more difficult, however, by the lack of surface indications of burials. Fortunately, there appear to be few unmounded burials for the population under study.

Unmounded burials

Three of the four Middle Woodland habitation sites extensively excavated by Struever in the lower Illinois Valley region yielded human skeletal remains. None were recovered from the Kamp habitation site (Struever 1960). Excavation of approximately 18,500 square feet of surface at the Apple Creek site produced four skeletons (Struever 1968c:299 and personal communication). One of these was an extended adult without burial associations, and the others (two of which were found in trash pits) were infants. Because of extensive disturbance of the Middle Woodland occupation by an early Late Woodland (White Hall) component, the burials could not be attributed to a specific occupation. Corwin (1968) identified two partial skeletons from Middle Woodland habitation areas of the Peisker site. One

of these, however, lay beneath a Middle Woodland mound, and the possibility that it is intrusive into earlier midden cannot be rejected. Much more extensive excavations at the Macoupin site produced a minimum of 8 and a maximum of 14 scattered human bone fragments assignable to the Middle Woodland occupation (Hill 1970). These remains represented a minimum of one individual.

Major investigations at Loy, a Middle Woodland habitation site in the tributary valley of Macoupin Creek, yielded no human bones and only two tooth fragments (Kenneth Farnsworth personal communication). Fragmentary skeletons of two infants, probably newly born, were recovered during the University of Illinois excavations at the Pool site (McGregor 1958:175); but since both Middle and Late Woodland sherds were found near these burials, their cultural affiliations are uncertain. The nearby Irving habitation site, with a small Middle Woodland component, yielded one burial; however, embedded in a rib and inside the body cavity were triangular Mississippi projectile points (McGregor 1958:177,179,181). At the multicomponent Ansell-Knight habitation site in the Mississippi Valley, 6 miles west of The Gardens of Kampsville, brief excavations by a University of Illinois field party yielded the skeleton of a child about 4 to 6 years of age, apparently in an indeterminate cultural context (McGregor 1958:174-175,178).

It is still premature to assume that mound burial was nearly universal. At the Snyders habitation site, located on the eastern margin of the Mississippi Valley, but only 3 miles from the lower Illinois Valley, 34 burials were found by amateur archeologist William Fecht in a 70-by-90-foot excavation area (Fecht 1961, 1969). The site is multicomponent, and the cultural affiliations of most of these burials are uncertain. Four were in an extended position, a typical but not exclusively Middle Woodland trait, and the remainder were reported as bundle burials. In a few cases, Hopewellian diagnostic artifacts were in apparent association, though the occurrence of the burials in a shallow, plow-disturbed midden leaves some doubt about the validity of these associations. One drilled Ohio pipestone bead (culturally diagnostic of Hopewell) was found with each of two burials, and with a third there occurred a fragmentary Hopewell vessel (Struever 1961:99). One other burial was encountered by Fecht in a Late Woodland pit.

Other writers have attributed burials within Snyders village to a Late Woodland occupation. According to James B. Griffin (1952:15-16)

Most of the occupation during the post-Hope-well was in the field north of the schoolhouse. In this area Jersey Bluff refuse pits and burials are clearly intrusive into the Hopewell period debris.

Gregory Perino (1952:10) suggested that—

The Hopewell buried in mounds on the ridges above the village, the bluff culture people buried at the edge of the terrace on which the village stood or were intrusive in the mounds or between the mounds on the ridges.

If Fecht's observations are reliable, it must be surmised that at least a few, though not all, of the burials in Snyders village were of Middle Woodland age. The proximity of this site to the lower Illinois Valley leaves open the possibility that at least a few sites in the study region may have similar burial areas. It is worth noting, however, that the information garnered informally from the many active relic collectors of the region does not confirm the possibility of extensive Middle Woodland burial in habitation sites.

Thus far no Middle Woodland burials have been discovered from locations other than mound groups or habitation areas, either individually or in cemeteries, though excavation of the Gibson and Pete Klunk mound groups disclosed that a few burials may be expected in natural knolls at the bluff crest between mounds (Buikstra 1972, Perino 1968).

Cremation

Extensive practice of cremation would cause serious underestimation of population size. For Ohio Hopewell, cremation was practiced frequent-ly; Shetrone (1930:98) estimated that 75 percent of the Hopewell burials recovered by the Ohio State Museum excavations were treated in this manner. The incidence is much lower, however, for Middle Woodland mound sites within the State of Illinois, and the lower Illinois Valley is con-sistent with this general trend. For other regions of the state, I have found reports of mass Middle Woodland cremation only from Ogden-Fettie Mound F°175, Liverpool Mound F°77, and pos-sibly Liverpool Mound F°79, in Fulton County (Hesselberth 1945, 1946; Cole and Deuel 1937: 134,143,173).

Appendix C provides detailed documentation on cremation in Middle Woodland mounds of the lower Illinois Valley. Such information demands careful evaluation because work done by amateurs and excavations conducted by archeologists prior to the development of a cultural chronology are often untrustworthy. Both Late Archaic and Late Woodland peoples cremated their dead more ex-tensively than did the Middle Woodland popula-tions of the region. Middle Woodland burial mounds sometimes occur in Archaic cemeteries; for example, in Pete Klunk Mound 7, Late Archaic burials and cremations were placed in a natural knoll and in a low capping mound, to be disturbed a thousand years later by the erection of a Middle Woodland mound (Perino 1968:67-94). Late Woodland burials often were placed intrusively into Middle Woodland mounds, and Late Wood-land secondary caps are sometimes placed over primary mounds dating to an earlier cultural period; e.g., Mounds 12 and 13 of the Pete Klunk group (Perino 1968:108-114). Careful excavation and reporting are imperative if complex events such as these are to be interpreted correctly.

To summarize Appendix C, cremations have been documented from 15 Middle Woodland mounds of the region; but only for Baehr Mound 1, the Robertson group (two mounds), and per-haps Kamp Mound 4, is there a possibility that excavators uncovered the cremated remains of numerous individuals. Unfortunately, the tech-niques of excavation and the field reports for these three early excavations leave important questions unanswered. For these mounds no estimate can be made of the number of individuals cremated. The crematory basins of the Robertson mounds pro-vide the best evidence for extensive cremation, but the cultural affiliation of this mound group is unknown.

Excluding the three possible instances of mass cremation, less than 2 percent of all Middle Woodland mound burials have been even partially burned.

Burial mounds need not be the site of crema-tion. Indeed, Late Woodland crematories not directly associated with mounds have been discov-ered in the lower Illinois Valley (Buikstra and Goldstein 1973). However, none are known for the Middle Woodland period, nor have any burnt skeletal remains been discovered in excavated habitation sites of the region. Therefore, we conclude tentatively that crematories and reposi-tories for the ashes are absent or rare outside the context of mound groups.

Variability in mortuary practices

The occurrence of intrasocietal variability in mortuary practices was the subject of a cross-cultural survey by Lewis R. Binford (1971), drawn from the Human Relations Area Files. This study identifies dimensions of social variability within societies which find expression in differential mortuary behavior—including multiple burial locations and differential treatment and disposition of the deceased. Moreover, it permits a rough assessment of the probabilities of linkage between various characteristics of the social persona and variations in mortuary ritual.

Forty societies were selected for the sample, covering a spectrum of nonstate societies that included hunter-gatherers, shifting and settled agriculturalists, and pastoralists. Binford proposed that the components of social persona that covary with mortuary practices are age, sex, social position, and social affiliation. In addition, the circumstances of cause or location of death sometimes are recognized by distinctive mortuary behavior. These might include deaths from warfare, epidemics, or other unexpected abnormal causes, or deaths occurring far from the base settlement.

Three of the distinctions in mortuary practices considered by Binford are relevant to the possibilities for an unmounded burial population in the lower Illinois Valley: (1) Treatment of the body, e.g., distinction by cremation or dismemberment; (2) disposition of the body, e.g., scaffold burial or disposal in the river, and (3) location of the grave. The distribution of these distinctions in the 40 societies in relation to aspects of the social persona is given in Table 7.

In few societies were cause or location of death the bases for differential treatment or disposition of the body or for variable grave location, and to the extent that the circumstances initiating alternative mortuary practices are "peculiar," they are

likely to involve only a small fraction of the total population. Furthermore, even if these distinctions were made in Middle Woodland societies, they might still be expressed within the context of mound burial. If the causes and location of death led, nonetheless, to the formation of a substantial unmounded mortuary subpopulation, then the age-sex distribution of the mound burials should show signs of biased representation; for while the age or sex of a person may be irrelevant for determining mortuary behavior when special contingencies of cause or location of death arise, it seems unlikely that the rate of occurrence of these circumstances would be independent of age or sex.

In a few cases, age of the deceased was recognized in mortuary practices, primarily in the location of the grave. For every case in which the variable dimension was grave location, infants and children were differentiated with respect to adults (Binford 1971:22). Children were buried either under house floors or in more peripheral locations than the adults. Not a single case was observed in which sex of the deceased resulted in distinctions along the mortuary dimensions relevant to our problem.

In 37.5 percent of the sample societies, grave location varied with respect to social affiliation (e.g., lineage and sodality membership). Thus, it is not improbable that Hopewellian societies in Illinois also maintained separate grave locations for some of their social subunits. Since a subunit such as a lineage may be expected to have an age-sex distribution approximating that of the entire society, a mound group burial population with an unbiased age distribution may deceptively represent only one or a few subunits of the society. However, Binford's sample also suggests that differential treatment or disposition of the body seldom varies with respect to social affiliation. Therefore, even if a fraction of the Middle Woodland population did not receive mound interment for reasons of social affiliation, it nevertheless is likely to have been buried rather than treated and processed in a radically different manner, such as by cremation, canoe burial, or scaffold burial. This reasoning is consistent with the lack of documentation for Middle Woodland cemeteries and individual graves outside mound contexts. More likely, if grave location varied with respect to lineage affiliation, it was a matter of burial in different mounds. Indeed, an association of mounds with lineages at Gibson-Klunk was proposed by Buikstra (1972) to account for the observation that males displayed more intermound

TABLE 7. *Some Characteristics of the Social Persona Recognized in Treatment of the Dead*[a]

Character- istics	Number of societies exhibiting covariation		
	Treatment of the body	Disposition of the body	Location of the grave
Cause of death	2	2	3
Location of death	1	1	0
Age	0	3	7
Sex	0	0	0
Social position	2	2	8
Social affiliation	2	1	15

[a]Based on a sample of 40 societies drawn from the Human Relations Area Files by Binford (1971:22).

genetic homogeneity than females. Plausibly, this biosocial patterning could have resulted from the simultaneous erection of mounds over a long period of time in which burial location was determined by female ties.

Another test of the possibility of alternative burial loci is suggested from Binford's study. In none of the 40 societies did the form or quantity of the burial furniture vary with social affiliation (Binford 1971:22). (Apparently, where social position was a function of social affiliation, e.g., as in stratified societies, Binford recorded concomitant mortuary variation as a function of social position rather than social affiliation.) Therefore, if Hopewellian societies of the lower Illinois Valley consisted of approximately egalitarian lineages, one could expect to find roughly the same grave furniture wherever the burials might be located. The aesthetic and economic value of Hopewellian craft items that appear in mortuary context is great enough to have sustained active searches for them by relic collectors through many years. However, items such as bear canine teeth, platform pipes, marine shells, and artifacts made from mica, copper, or obsidian have never been reported by collectors or archeologists from locations other than mounds or villages. At the same time, numerous isolated finds of plummets—another artifact prized by collectors—have been documented (Goldstein n.d.). This suggests that the lack of reports for isolated finds of these artifact types is not a result of poor communication between relic collectors and archeologists. If indeed these goods were distributed with Middle Woodland burials without regard to burial location, then there is strong evidence against the occurrence of unmounded Middle Woodland cemeteries or numerous isolated burials as yet unknown to archeologists. The occasional occurrence of such artifacts in villages, very rarely in evident burial association, is undoubtedly a reflection of their functioning in social contexts wider than the mortuary sphere (Struever 1964:88). Nor are any villages known where such materials are concentrated in a restricted area, as might be expected if burial areas existed.

It remains to consider variable mortuary practices as a function of social position. In relatively few societies were linkages observed between social position and the treatment or disposition of the body, but in 20 percent of them burial location varied with respect to social position. Positions that are *achieved* may be expected to correlate strongly with age and sex even when there are no explicit age or sex requirements for holding them. Thus, a substantial unmounded subpopulation consisting of individuals with special achieved status would be expected to leave a recognizable age-sex bias in the mound population. *Ascribed* social status, however, is more likely to be based on kinship affiliation, cutting across all age-sex lines. Thus, for instance, members of lineages in a low social position could be denied mound burial without affecting the age-sex distribution of the mound burials. In 21 of the 40 societies, Binford found that the form or quantity of the grave furniture varied with social position. Thus, a low-status, unmounded burial population could conceivably be marked by none of the distinctive Hopewellian craft items found in the mounds and villages. It would be particularly difficult to interpret correctly a situation in which the bones of individuals of low ascribed status were destroyed without a trace.

Against this possibility is the rather weak evidence obtained from the lower Illinois Valley for social stratification and for correlated phenomena such as craft specialization, economic surpluses, and major trade in luxury items. A comparison of Illinois and Ohio Hopewell in terms of Service's criteria (1962:143) for a chiefdom level of social integration led Struever (1965:212-214) to conclude that the two cultures were organized on different levels of complexity. According to Struever, evidence for the conformance of Illinois Hopewell to chiefdom organization is slight.

Flanders and Griffin (1970:187,188) remark that "if burial in mounds is *ipso facto* because of some status position in the society it is not clear what the status was." They could see no evidence at the Knight mound group that artifact classes reflected more than a division of labor "with some emphasis on males as those concerned with supernatural affairs, perhaps through medicine bundles with pipes and raptorial bird remains for example"; nor was internal evidence of priestly or ruling hierarchies obvious to them. For the Gibson-Klunk mounds, Buikstra (1972:136) also concluded that internal evidence was not reflective of kinship-based status positions: "Culturally determined locus of burial has no pan-mound referent in the biological system. . . . On the basis of all sources of information, it appears that personal attributes—such as strength and physical abilities—were more important than kin association in determining the amount and kind of attention accorded the individual at death."

With rare exceptions, status reinforcement through *ostentatious* display of exotic grave goods with burials does not occur in lower Illinois Valley mounds. (See App. D for references to mound reports.) Indeed, the cumulative number of Hopewell interaction sphere items recovered from mortuary sites in the lower Illinois Valley is modest, particularly in comparison with those in Ohio (cf. Struever and Houart 1972: Table 1).

Systematic variation reflective of status differences undoubtedly can be discovered by conjunctive studies of the form, diversity, and quantity of grave goods, of burial location in and between mounds, of burial orientation, etc. But such differences do not necessarily translate primarily into a *hierarchical* status arrangement with vast differences between the lower and upper positions.

Though Hopewell interaction sphere goods functioning within the social subsystem ("sociotechnic items") were garnered over a vast area of the continent, large labor inputs and specialized economic institutions were not necessarily required for introducing them into the lower Illinois Valley. As previously noted, the quantities of these materials in grave association are relatively small, and the evidence from village sites, as yet evaluated only subjectively, does not suggest the movement of large quantities of these materials. Griffin (1965:146-147), for example, suggests that all of the obsidian appearing in the Midwest during the Middle Woodland period could conceivably have been brought from Wyoming in a single trip. The quantities are particularly unimpressive when a mean annual rate of introduction is considered by dividing the totals by 550 years, the length of the Middle Woodland period.

Some archeologists have been of the opinion that since only a few individuals were buried in mounds, there must have been a large supportive population to erect them. However, even though past mound excavations in the lower Illinois Valley have often been of lamentable quality, they have produced a mean of 15 individuals per mound (discussed later in this chapter); the mean would be considerably higher had all burials been recovered. Thus, even without a supportive population, each member of the Middle Woodland community would have been required to construct, on the average, no more than 1/15 of an entire mound during his lifetime.

The existence of a Middle Woodland agriculture has been another reason for proposing considerable social complexity. However, analysis of plant

and animal remains, largely collected by flotation techniques, from a number of lower Illinois Valley sites have led to the suggestion that agriculture was of minor importance during that time and that intensive harvesting of plant seeds and backwater fish populations provided the major contrast with the Early Woodland subsistence base (Struever 1968b:221-226, 1968c; Rackerby 1969).

In the context of this paper, I can do little more than state my opinions regarding Middle Woodland social organization. However, with respect to the proposal of a highly stratified society, numerous testable hypotheses can be generated—hypotheses that are independent of the assumptions underlying population estimation. Therefore, the matter need not remain indefinitely within the realm of speculation. And, of course, even if such stratification existed, low-status individuals may still have received mound burial. Struever and Houart (1972:61) speculate that Middle Woodland mound cemeteries in the floodplain, in particular the six groups dominated by one or two large loaf-shaped mounds, may also have been "focal points of economic-political-ritual activities." If such was the case, burials in these cemeteries may well represent a social group with special supracommunity status.

In sum, the empirical evidence suggests a preponderance of Middle Woodland burials in mounds and a low incidence of mortuary practices destructive of skeletal material. The age-sex distribution in the mound population provides one important test of the proposition that most individuals received mound burial, and the biases inferred thus far do not lead to its rejection. Binford's cross-cultural study of differential mortuary practices suggested some correlated social contingencies, which led to further refinement of test implications.

Mound destruction by natural agency

More possibilities for undercounting the regional mortuary population arise from the physical destruction of mounds either by natural geomorphological processes or by man. First consider the potential for natural destruction. Middle Woodland mound groups are located almost exclusively on bluff crests overlooking the Illinois Valley and in the valley floodplain (cf. Struever 1968b: App.). In the former location, significant erosion will not occur if the natural vegetation cover remains or if the land is devoted to pasture. Steep slopes generally prevent plowing and crop raising. Consequently, modern erosion seldom threatens bluff-crest mounds.

However, on the valley floor, migration of the river channel can easily destroy mound groups. Direct evidence for such destruction would usually be lacking of course, but in the opinion of the geologist William Rubey (1952:123), who surveyed the geology and mineral resources of the Hardin and Brussels Geological Survey Quadrangles, the Illinois River has been "remarkably stable" since well before historic times. The Illinois River is not a meandering stream with attendant cutting and filling. Rubey suggests that the high natural levees of the present river channel resulted from repeated additions of alluvium and that the absence of bars and swales in the floodplain indicates that the river has long been in its present position. The occurrence of Middle Woodland mounds on natural levees adjacent to the present river channel suggests that at least in part the channel takes the same course that it followed 2000 years ago.

Though the river course is for the most part stable, mounds constructed on levees adjacent to the river channel may be subject to considerable local cutting. For instance, in 1929, J. L. B. Taylor observed partial erosion of Naples-Abbott Mound 1 down the riverbank (Griffin and Morgan 1941:29), though the destruction has progressed no further since that time. Mound 6 of the Naples-Castle group is also eroded by river action. The Peisker habitation site and mound group lie on a natural levee adjacent to the present channel. Though cultural debris is scattered over more than 500 feet parallel to the river, in many places the scatter is only 30 feet wide. High densities are found at the edge of the bank, and in all probability some of the levee has been cut away since the period of prehistoric occupation, perhaps destroying mounds as well as part of the habitation area. No other examples are known for the lower Illinois Valley where changes in the channel may have destroyed mounds.

Because of alluviation in the floodplain, combined with plowing, some low mounds may not rise above the present ground surface, hence making them difficult to discover. For example, test excavations in seven mounds of the Kamp group revealed that the ground surface is now at least 2 feet higher than at the time of construction (Griffin and Morgan 1941:36).

On the whole, it is unlikely that many entire mound groups have been destroyed by natural phenomena.

Mound destruction by man

Most burial mounds in the Midwest have been opened by relic collectors. Nonetheless, these uncontrolled excavations may not pose insuperable difficulties for a population estimate. The problem can be approached by determining the number of Middle Woodland mounds and the mean number of burials per mound separately, under the supposition that enough reasonably well preserved mounds exist to permit a reliable approximation for the mean burial population size for all mounds.

Many mounds of the region apparently suffering total destruction of cultural data have proven very productive in recent excavations. The Gibson-Klunk mounds provide a case in point. (See Sect. 2 for an evaluation of the disturbance there resulting from the largely undocumented early excavations.) Inexperienced excavators sometimes fail to dig deeply enough to reach the original ground surface or do not recognize the outlines of subfloor burial pits. Usually the center of the mound is pitted in search of a tomb which may, however, be situated off-center. Multiple tombs may also defeat this strategy. Pitting in a mound probably "immunizes" it against subsequent disturbances. Until a few years ago, even professional archeologists generally missed discovering peripheral burials. Thus, with careful mound excavation, it should often be possible to set reasonable limits upon the effects of previous disturbance.

Another question is whether enough mounds have survived to permit a meaningful count of them. Mound groups, by definition, are less susceptible to total destruction than individual mounds. For this reason, the total number of Middle Woodland mound groups and the mean number of mounds in a Middle Woodland group are determined separately in this paper, thus enabling estimation of the latter variable under more controlled conditions.

Since the bottomland mounds are located on prime farmland, they are more likely to be leveled or removed than are the bluff-crest mounds. The frequent occurrence of submound tombs gives grounds for optimism that even leveled mound groups could be detected by a careful survey. However, the preponderance of bluff-crest mounds cannot be explained by a differentially higher rate of mound destruction in the floodplain. Even in the 1800's when the bottoms were largely devoid of cultivation because of poor drainage, it was noted that mounds were more numerous in bluff-crest locations (McAdams 1884:685; Snyder 1883; Mitchell 1880; Middleton 1888).

In sum, my position is that a fairly reliable count of mound groups can be made. A careful survey of historical resources for the area (e.g., newspaper accounts, interviews, early aerial photography, personal papers), to ascertain instances of mound excavation or removal could further test this proposition.

Number of Mound Groups

The remaining undetermined variables are the number of mound groups in the lower Illinois Valley M and the average number of individuals per group $\bar{N}$. Estimates of M and $\bar{N}$, though rough, will permit the construction of a probable range for population size.

First the need and feasibility of a complete mound survey and of more mound excavation is assessed. For a survey to be effective, Middle Woodland mounds must be distinguished from those dating to other time periods. Mound location in itself can suggest cultural affiliation. Archaic and Late Woodland mounds were rarely or never built in the Illinois Valley floodplain where Middle Woodland mounds are more commonly found. However, Archaic, Middle Woodland, Late Woodland, and Mississippi mounds are all found on the bluff crests overlooking the valley and must therefore be distinguished. Furthermore, mounds of a single group are usually culturally heterogeneous, so that excavation in one does not indicate the cultural affiliations of the others.

According to Gregory Perino, who has excavated many mounds in the region, an accurate prediction of cultural affiliation can be made from knowledge of external mound morphology, size, and location on the blufftop (Perino 1968:11). His criteria have yet to be subjected to controlled testing, but even if they were, for example, only 80 percent successful, a complete mound survey would substantially improve the reliability of population estimation. (Such a program for intensive survey of mounds on the lower Illinois Valley bluffline is now in progress under the supervision of Jane Buikstra, Northwestern Univeristy.)

Should morphological and locational criteria prove insufficiently diagnostic of cultural affiliation, the fraction of all prehistoric mounds assignable to the Middle Woodland period can still be estimated from the information provided by excavations. But since a biased and relatively small sample is available for estimating this fraction, its upper and lower limits can only be specified within a wide range.

One serious problem for an estimate of the number of Middle Woodland mounds is that Middle Woodland and early Late Woodland (White Hall phase) mounds have not yet been distinguished either by external appearance or by excavation. Although a gradual shift of mortuary practices from classic Hopewell to Late Woodland Jersey Bluff is well documented (Struever 1960:123-150), no mound containing White Hall ceramics has been reported from the lower Illinois Valley. In the adjacent Mississippi Valley, early Late Woodland pottery (Canteen) of Fox Creek phase has been discovered in association with burials in the Knight (Griffin *et al.* 1970) and Joe Gay mounds (Cook 1971). Also, at the latter mound group there is evidence of White Hall (early Late Woodland) affiliation (Cook 1971:29). Griffin (personal communication) observes that vessel $C^{\circ}2$-15 (from Knight Mound 2) has Weaver White Hall characteristics (Griffin *et al.* 1970: 26-27, Pl. 16b-17a). He also attributes some of the Jersey Bluff mounds excavated by Titterington (1935) in Jersey County to Fox Creek phase (1970:10).

If careful and complete excavations in the future do not permit adequate differentiation of White Hall mounds from those of earlier cultural phases, it may be expedient to extend the time-span of the population estimate to include the early Late Woodland period. This would not be purely arbitrary because there is much evidence that early Late Woodland pottery and projectile point styles developed from local antecedents. Surface surveys by the Northwestern University Archeological Program suggest that White Hall settlement patterns are more similar to those of Middle Woodland phases than to Jersey Bluff; and early Late Woodland subsistence was still largely tied to a hunting-gathering base.

Information now available permits a provisional estimate of the number of Middle Woodland mound groups in the lower Illinois Valley region. The method involves extrapolating the total number within the 2,880-square-mile research area from the known frequency of groups in restricted parts of the valley. It must be emphasized that questions concerning the "reality" of prehistoric groupings are irrelevant to the aims of this study. Mound groups may be quite arbitrarily defined as census units of convenience. Also it should be noted that what is estimated is not the total number of groups in the region but rather the number of groups having at least one Middle Woodland mound.

Twenty-seven mound groups in the region have been attributed in part to the Middle Woodland period (Fig. 1). Most are distributed along the bluffs on the western margin of the Illinois Valley or on the floodplain a short distance from the present-day river channel. They are highly clustered, a patterning which relates in part to where archeological investigations have centered. By determining the mean north-south distance between mound groups within the clusters, the total number of Middle Woodland mound groups occurring on the western side of the valley or near the Illinois River can be estimated. Within the mound group cluster areas listed below, archeological investigations have been intensive, if not systematic. Consequently, the within-cluster site densities should be fairly reliable. The clusters include the following mound groups (the numbering corresponds to that of the map in Fig. 1): 9-10-12-13; 32-35-38-39-40-42; 53-55-59-62; 73-74-76; 77-78-80; 83-84. The mean distance between mound groups in the clusters is 1.20 miles, leading to an estimated 67/1.20 = 56 mound groups in the 67-mile length of the lower valley.

Since only three Middle Woodland mound groups are documented from the eastern valley margin, the total number of groups there cannot be estimated reliably by the projection procedure used for the west side. The lower frequency on the east side of the valley is not readily explained as the consequence of less intensive archeological investigation. Gregory Perino (1968:11) observes that

[Middle Woodland mound] groups exist in or near most of the hollows and creeks that enter the river flood plains both up and down stream. These groups are situated almost exclusively on the west side of the river to as far north as Naples. From this point northward to Meredosia, the mounds are grouped or strung out on high sand ridges on the east side near the river.

In Jersey County, which is located east of the river at the south end of the research universe, Paul F. Titterington investigated many mound groups over a period of years (over 1,000 burials excavated). Except for a miniscule quantity of Middle Woodland remains, the mounds dated entirely to Late Woodland-Mississippi time periods (Titterington 1935; Shalkop 1949).

Middle Woodland village sites also occur in lower frequency on the eastern valley margin. Applying the cluster method to villages (see Sect.

2, this chapter, for calculations), 54 Middle Woodland villages were estimated for locations west of the river or near the river on the east side and 32 were projected in locations near the eastern valley margin. The ratio of western to eastern villages, then, is 1.7:1. Thus, if the true mound group to village ratio is roughly the same throughout the valley, a total of (56/54) X 32 = 33 mound groups can be predicted for the eastern bluffs, giving an estimated 89 groups for the lower Illinois Valley proper and its adjacent bluff crests.

Neither relic collectors nor archeologists have considered the secondary valleys and uplands in the lower Illinois Valley region a fertile zone for Middle Woodland mounds. In fact, only one Middle Woodland mound group has been documented for the secondary valleys—the Gracey site, located on a blufftop overlooking Macoupin Creek 30 miles from the Illinois Valley (Farnsworth 1973). The generally low density and small size of habitation sites in the secondary valleys (see Sect. 2, this chap.) suggest a sparse Middle Woodland occupational density in comparison with the main valley. Though an exact estimate of the frequency of Middle Woodland mound groups in the minor valleys cannot presently be made, I consider 10 groups a generous allowance. An estimate of 100 Middle Woodland mound groups within the entire research area thus seems reasonable. My opinion is that the figure will prove to be lower because (1) undoubtedly the observed clustering of mounds is in part a real patterning, and (2) the number of mound groups estimated for the eastern valley margin disregards the evidence for a very low Middle Woodland mound density in that zone. A mound group total exceeding 120 could occur only if the present sample is giving a highly misleading impression of their frequency.

Size of Burial Populations

Table 8 records the mean size of the burial mound mortuary populations that would accompany a given hypothetical level of the Middle Woodland regional population. The relationship is calculated over a range of possible values for the number of mound groups in the region. The table is based on an evaluation of Equation (4-3), using 29.19 years as the mean lifespan and 550 years as the length of the Middle Woodland period. To obtain the mean size of a mound group population, two factors are estimated separately:

1. The mean number of individuals per mound.

TABLE 8. *Relationship Between Mean Number of Individuals per Mound Group, Number of Mound Groups, and Population Size in the Lower Illinois Valley Region During the Middle Woodland Period*

Population size	Population density (per sq mi)		Required number of individuals per mound group for a specified regional population level						
	1,000-sq-mi research universe	2,880-sq-mi research universe	Number of mound groups						
			50	60	80	100	120	140	160
100	0.10	0.035	37.7	31.4	23.6	18.8	15.7	13.5	11.8
288	.29	.1	109	90.4	67.8	54.3	45.2	38.8	33.9
576	.58	.2	217	181	136	109	90.4	77.5	67.8
864	.87	.3	326	271	203	163	136	116	102
1,152	1.2	.4	434	362	271	217	181	155	136
1,440	1.4	.5	543	452	339	271	226	194	170
2,160	2.2	.75	814	678	509	407	339	291	254
2,880	2.9	1	1,090	904	678	543	452	388	339
5,760	5.8	2	2,170	1,810	1,360	1,090	904	775	678
14,400	14.4	5	5,430	4,520	3,390	2,710	2,260	1,940	1,700
28,800	28.8	10	10,900	9,040	6,780	5,430	4,520	3,880	3,390

2. The number of mounds per group.

This two-step procedure is necessary because entire mound groups have seldom been excavated.

Early excavations provide virtually no reliable counts of mound populations. Traditional digging techniques were not oriented toward the recovery of entire burial populations. Excavators typically were more interested in the burial furniture than the skeletal material, and until biological anthropologists turned toward population approaches, the recovery of entire populations was not an important concern. Bones are often so badly decayed that inexperienced excavators cannot remove and may even fail to observe them. Careless digging and impressionistic reporting often prevent exact counts of even the *excavated* individuals. For example, reports often stated only that "several" or "many" individuals were discovered at some location in a mound. We were consistently conservative in counting and assigning a Middle Woodland affiliation to individuals, to assure that a reliable lower bound for the regional population level could be established. Thus, in the example above, a minimum count of two individuals would be used. Since skeletons are often partially or totally disarticulated (Buikstra 1972), casual digging and description cannot yield accurate counts. Another source of error has been the hasty characterization of peripherally located skeletons as intrusive burials from a later cultural period.

The traditional approach to excavation was to sink a single pit into the center of a mound in search of a central tomb or to trench toward the center from one end. Thus, much of a mound was bypassed—in particular, the peripheral parts. Recent careful and thorough excavations at the Klunk, Peisker, and Gibson mound groups have recovered many individuals scattered over the original ground surface, or interred in subfloor pits (Perino 1968, 1966; Buikstra 1972). At the Peisker mound group, for instance, most of the burials from one mound were around its circumference.

Because of these systematic errors, the mean number of individuals *counted* in mound groups is a very conservative minimum estimate of the true average.

Nonetheless, even within the same group, mounds have a wide range of variation in numbers of individuals, ranging from zero to a high thus far of about 120. This range, for instance, existed within the carefully and completely excavated Pete Klunk group. Consequently, it is dangerous to discard low mound counts while accepting high ones. Burial data from a few very minor or very incompletely reported excavations will not be used, however, in constructing the minimum population estimate. Some control over self-serving decisions in data screening is established by ruling that individual excavated mounds in a group cannot be excluded from consideration. A mound group is accepted or rejected entirely. Excluded mound groups are those in the Naples cluster, Merodosia-Hilderbrand, Hagen, Gracey, Hazelherst, and Meppen.

For the mounds listed in Table 9, the mean count was 15.0 persons with a standard error of 2.6. Data used in the computations are tabulated in more detail in Appendix D. Because of the

TABLE 9. *Minimum Number of Middle Woodland Individuals Excavated From Mound Groups of the Lower Illinois Valley Region*

Mound group	Mounds	Minimum number of individuals
Baehr	1-2, 4	14
Bedford	1, 4, 8-12	82
Brangenberg	1-3	22
Tom Collins	1	16
Duncan Farm	No number	5
Gibson	1-6, Knoll C	161
Hardin	1	4
Helm	1	2
Kamp	2-4, 9	13
Pete Klunk	1-2, 5-7, 11-13	375
Knight	3-8, 16, 22	110
L'Orient	1-2	53
Merrigan	1	3
Montezuma	1-12, 14-15	69
Parsell	199	5
Peisker	1-3	58
Pilot's Peak	1, 3	9
Swartz	1	3
Total	68	1,004

TABLE 10. *Number of Mounds per Group in the Lower Illinois Valley Region, for Groups With at Least One Middle Woodland Mound*

Mound group	Number of mounds[a]	Probable number of Middle Woodland mounds[b]
Baehr	5	4?
Bedford	16	13?
Brangenberg	3	3
Tom Collins	2	1
Gibson	7	6
Gracey	5	–
Hardin	5	–
Hazelherst	8	–
Helm	6	3
Kamp	10	10?
Pete Klunk	12	8
Knight Mounds 1-13	13	⩾6
Knight Mounds 16-26	11	3?
L'Orient	2	2
Meppen	12	11?
Meredosia-Hilderbrand	13	–
Merrigan	4	–
Montezuma	14	14?
Mound House	3	–
Naples Abbott	9	–
Naples Castle	2	2?
Naples Chambers	5	5?
Parsell	10	1
Peisker	3	3
Pilot's Peak	5	5?
Robertson	2	–
Swartz	3	–
Number of Groups = 27	$\Sigma = 190$	ca. 100 of 138 (72%)

[a]Mound groups omitted if number of mounds is in question.

[b]No estimate attempted if excavation information on mound morphology is very limited; question marks omitted only if all mounds were excavated and all yielded definitive evidence of cultural affiliation.

haphazard nature of the mound sample, the standard error cannot be translated into an objective estimate of sample reliability. Nevertheless, it gives a rough approximation of the level of error that may be expected due to sample size only. In comparison with the expected level of systematic error, this "small sample error" is minor, and since systematic errors are in the direction of undercounting, the mean of 15.0 persons per mound may be confidently retained as a lower bound for the true value.

Number of Mounds per Group

To complete the estimate of the mean size $\bar{N}$ of a mound group burial population, it is necessary to know the mean number of Middle Woodland mounds in a group. In Table 10, mound group sizes are listed for groups *with at least one* documented Middle Woodland mound. The table is based primarily upon the summaries of Struever (1968b: App. I and personal communication); also Griffin, Flanders, and Titterington (1970), Buikstra (1972), and Farnsworth (1973 and personal communication). The mean of 7.04 mounds per group (standard error = 0.83), calculated from the 27 groups listed in Table 10, is too large as an estimate of the mean number of *Middle Woodland* mounds because other mounds of a single group were often constructed during two or more time periods. Usually, the cultural affiliation of a mound can be determined by excavation, but few mound groups are completely excavated. Had mounds of the region been selected at random for excavation, one could estimate the mean number of Middle Woodland mounds per group as

(Number of mds./gp.) $\times$ (% Middle Woodland mds. in excavated sample)

However, past excavations have been strongly biased toward mounds having an external morphology suggestive of a Middle Woodland origin. To circumvent this bias, the number of Middle Woodland mounds per group was estimated from a subset of 18 mound groups in which all mounds could be sorted into "probable Middle Woodland" affiliation or "probable non-Middle Woodland" affiliation from the evidence of excavation or from external mound morphology (see Table 10). For this estimate, a circular blufftop mound is regarded as Middle Woodland in origin and an elliptical blufftop mound as non-Middle Woodland. (See App. D for a summary of mound dimensions.) It should be emphasized that no mound group is included in this subset unless it has at least one "proven," i.e., excavated, Middle Woodland mound.

A mean of 5.56 Middle Woodland mounds is obtained for the 18 groups containing documented Middle Woodland mounds; 72.5 percent of the 138 mounds in this sample were of putative Middle Woodland origin.

The estimate may be improved, however, by calculating it as a *two-phase ratio mean* (Kish 1965:446-447), i.e., by multiplying the percentage of Middle Woodland mounds obtained in the sample of 18 groups by the mean obtained for the number of mounds per group (all components) in the larger sample. Thus, the adjusted mean number of Middle Woodland mounds is 0.725 × 7.04 = 5.10. The standard error of the two-phase ratio mean is 0.81, which is less than the error accompanying the simple mean (see Kish 1965:447 for method of computation). To allow for uncertainties attributable to the small size of the sample, we shall use the mean reduced by one standard error, i.e., 4.3, as a minimum estimate of Middle Woodland mounds per group. This is appropriate for use in a minimum estimate of population size.

The direction and magnitude of systematic errors in estimating the mean number of Middle Woodland mounds per group is not evident.

A Minimum Population Estimate

Minimum values of 4.3 Middle Woodland mounds per group and 15.0 burials per mound provide a minimum of $\bar{N}$ = 4.3 × 15.0 = 64 Middle Woodland burials per mound group. Thus, we now have estimates for all the variables—M, $\bar{N}$, $\bar{A}$, and L—entering into the population formula (4-3). However, before proceeding with the computations, a few more remarks can be made about possible errors associated with mean life span $\bar{A}$.

The value of $\bar{A}$ = 29.19 years is obtained from the statistics of the Gibson-Klunk burial population. Regarding the skeletal series from these mounds as a sample from the regional population of Middle Woodland burials, one may calculate a

standard error. Its value of 0.94 is small enough in comparison with the mean to enable us to disregard the small sample error without serious consequences.

Systematic errors in estimating $\bar{A}$ have several sources. First, suppose age data were available for all burials recovered from the lower Illinois Valley. What biases are predicted for this haphazard sample? Because infant skeletons are more fragile and poorly preserved than older skeletons, the major bias in respect to age is likely to be against the very young. The effect of this is to raise the mean age of death of the population that is recovered. Nevertheless, the total effect of the bias against infants must be to *underestimate* the total number of man-years lived; that is, the elevation of mean age among the excavated burials is more than compensated by the lower count of individuals. Careful excavation and good bone preservation of burials recovered from the Gibson-Klunk mounds favor a lower mean life span than among those of most other sites. Another source of bias is the extent to which Gibson-Klunk is unrepresentative of lower Illinois Valley burial populations. Very little reliable information is available about other burial populations and at present we cannot assess the direction of bias. Systematic error may also arise from the assessment of age (see discussion of age evaluation in Buikstra 1972), and again we cannot predict the direction of bias. One may note, however, that the mean age of 30 years obtained for the Klunk Hopewell population by King B. Hunter (Blakely 1971) compares favorably with Buikstra's mean for the combined Gibson-Klunk population. If bias is present and significant, it is common to both evaluations. In sum, to the extent that it is possible to assess the

TABLE 11. *Minimum Population Estimates, Based on Mean of 64 Excavated Middle Woodland Burials per Mound Group*

Number of mound groups	Size of population	Population density (per sq mi)	
		1,000-sq-mi research universe	2,880-sq-mi research universe
60	204	0.20	0.07
80	272	.27	.09
100	340	.34	.12
120	408	.41	.14
140	476	.48	.17
160	543	.54	.19

systematic errors, the tendency is toward under-estimation of the true value of $\bar{A}$.

Table 11 records a series of estimates of population size and density for a range of possible values of the number of mound groups M. For the preferred value of $M = 100$ groups, the total population size is 340, a density of 0.34 persons per square mile over the smaller 1,000-square-mile research area (slightly less if the more distant mound groups in secondary valleys are deducted) or only 0.12 persons per square miles over the 2,880-square-mile region. Though it is a safe base for the population estimate, it is not very useful because of the numerous minimizing assumptions.

A Maximum Population Estimate

Assuming that most of the Middle Woodland people were buried in mounds, a maximum estimate for the regional population may be computed from mound group data. The 375 individuals recovered from the completely excavated Pete Klunk mound group constitute the largest burial population yet recovered in the region. The mean of 47 individuals per mound of Middle Woodland origin in this group is higher than any other, and of its total of 12 mounds, 8 are of Middle Woodland origin, in comparison with the regional mean of 7.04 mounds for *all* components. Thus, with near certainty the *mean* Middle Woodland mound group burial population is less than 375. In Table 12, a series of models for the maximum population level are presented. They are based upon a mean of 390 individuals per group and a range of possible values for the number of mound groups. The higher figure of 390 burials was used to allow for minor disturbance in the Pete Klunk mounds prior to Perino's excavations. (Sect. 2, this chapter, discusses the extent of disturbance.)

TABLE 12. *Population Estimates, Based on a Mean of 390 Middle Woodland Burials per Mound Group*

Number of mound groups	Size of population	Population density (per sq mi)	
		1,000-sq-mi research universe	2,880-sq-mi research universe
60	1,240	1.2	0.43
80	1,660	1.7	.57
100	2,070	2.1	.72
120	2,480	2.5	.86
140	2,900	2.9	1.00
160	3,310	3.3	1.15

Even with the maximal values of 160 Middle Woodland mound groups and 390 individuals per group, the corresponding population density throughout the 2,880-square-mile region would have been only 1.15 persons per square mile, for a total of 3,310 persons. In the more reasonable range of 80 to 120 mound groups, a density range of 0.57 to 0.86 persons per square mile is obtained as the upper limit to population in the larger research universe, or a total of 1,660 to 2,480 individuals.

The Missing Burials

Thus far, my procedure has been to calculate population levels on the assumption that all individuals were buried in mounds. The reasoning can also be reversed to obtain the percentage of individuals who must be missing from mounds if a specified, hypothetical population level is to be attained.

In this section, an exact estimate of the mean size of a mound burial population will be used, one which is based on information from only the best-controlled mound excavations. These include the Pete Klunk and Gibson mounds, Kamp Mound 9, and Peisker Mound 2. With allowances for incomplete excavation and previous disturbance (see App. D and Sect. 2, this chapter) the mean burial population of these 16 mounds was 38 individuals. Multiplying this figure by the estimated average of 5.1 Middle Woodland mounds in a group gives a mean burial population of 194 individuals per group.

Table 13 indicates the proportion of deceased receiving mound burial for various hypothetical levels of the regional population and for different mound group frequencies. Mean size of mound group burial populations is a constant (194 individuals) in the table. Blank cells indicate that the hypothetical population level is achieved or exceeded from the contribution of mounded burials and that no missing subpopulation need be assumed. To illustrate use of the table, suppose the region contains 100 mounds. Population densities of less than 0.36 persons per square mile in the 2,880-square-mile region do not imply alternatives to mound interment for disposal of the deceased. But if the density were 5 persons per square mile, then only 7.2 percent of the deceased could have received mound burial. Even a one-in-three rate of interment would provide a population density just greater than 1 individual per square mile.

TABLE 13. *Percentage of All Middle Woodland Deceased Buried in Lower Illinois Valley Mounds, for a Range of Plausible Population Levels (Based on an Estimate of 194 Individuals per Mound Group)*

Size of population	Population density (per sq mi)		Percentage of individuals buried in mounds for a hypothetical population size[a]						
	1,000-sq-mi research universe	2,880-sq-mi research universe	Number of mound groups						
			50	60	80	100	120	140	160
			Number of mounds (assuming 5.1 mounds/group)						
			255	306	408	510	612	714	816
100	0.1	0.035	x	x	x	x	x	x	x
288	.29	.1	x	x	x	x	x	x	x
576	.58	.2	89	x	x	x	x	x	x
864	.87	.3	60	72	95	x	x	x	x
1,152	1.2	.4	45	54	72	89	x	x	x
1,440	1.4	.5	36	43	57	72	86	x	x
2,160	2.2	.75	24	29	38	48	57	67	76
2,880	2.9	1	18	21	29	36	43	50	57
5,760	5.8	2	8.9	11	14	18	21	25	29
14,400	14.4	5	3.6	4.3	5.5	7.2	8.6	10	11
28,800	28.8	10	1.8	2.1	2.9	3.6	4.3	5.0	5.7

[a]An "x" indicates that 194 burials per mound group are sufficient to account for hypothetical population level.

2. THE MOUND-VILLAGE CALIBRATION METHOD

The Mound-Village Calibration method is predicted upon the existence of mound groups, in association with specific village sites, that serve as repositories for the remains of most individuals from the villages. In making this population estimate, it is assumed that the deceased of The Gardens of Kampsville were interred in the blufftop Gibson-Klunk mounds overlooking the village. Perino and Buikstra excavated a total of 533 Middle Woodland individuals who lived an estimated 15,557 to 16,091 man-years, the number varying according to one's choice of mortality models for old adults (see Chap. 3, Sect. 3). I shall use the smaller figure in the succeeding calculations, but should the larger be more accurate, the error is minimal.

If the village was stationary in size, then the number of man-years lived by members of the community while the burial population accumulated was also 15,557.* For a local population estimate, one must solve for population size in the equation

Mean village population size X length of occupation = 15,557

For instance, occupation of The Gardens of Kampsville by a community of 15,557 individuals

*This relationship also holds for a population which fluctuates because of migration, provided that the age structure of the population remains stable.

for just 1 year could have resulted in the number of deaths observed in the burial population; 1,556 persons for 10 years; 156 for 100 years; etc. A series of possible solutions is given in Table 14.

Other attempts at estimating local population size (e.g., Howells 1960:170-171; Jamison 1971: 123) have obtained man-years, though implicitly, by means of the formula

$$\text{Man-years} = \frac{\text{number of burials}}{\text{crude death rate}}$$

where the death rate was based upon ethnographic analogy with historic Indian groups. More reliable results are obtained by drawing upon information provided by the age structure of the prehistoric burial population and then calculating man-years

TABLE 14. *Length of Occupation Versus Population Size of The Gardens of Kampsville, Based on 533 Burials From Two Mound Groups*

Length of occupation (years)	Village size (inhabitants)
1	15,557
5	3,111
10	1,556
25	622
50	311
100	156
150	104
200	78
320	49
550	28
690	23

as the sum of ages at death or, equivalently, as the number of burials times mean age at death $\bar{A}$.

The major problem encountered in basing a local population estimate upon statistics of the burial population is that knowledge of the length of occupation is of the same order of uncertainty as the population size that one is attempting to estimate. Only two or three chronological subdivisions of Middle Woodland in the lower Illinois Valley have been proposed with any confidence (Struever 1968b:158-159; Griffin 1970). Large sites often have long histories of habitation; however, it would be nearly impossible to distinguish between continuous and intermittent occupation over a number of years and, in the latter case, even more difficult to measure the length of habitation.

Relationship of Regional Population Density to Village Occupation

The confounding of *local* population size and length of occupation is of no consequence to a regional estimate averaged over a long time period, since an estimate of man-years is all that is required of each local situation. It will be convenient to calculate the *mean* annual contribution of each village site to the regional Middle Woodland population density, including those years when the site was unoccupied. Within the smaller 1,000-square-mile research universe, The Gardens of Kampsville contributed a mean of $15,557/(550 \times 1,000) = 0.028$ persons per square mile during the entire Middle Woodland period. Thus, for instance, 3.5 villages in a region having the same "quantity" of occupation (15,557 man-years) as The Gardens of Kampsville would maintain a regional population density of 0.1 person per

square mile; 35 would maintain 1 person per square mile; etc. Note that this method of calculation requires no assumptions about the contemporaneity of the villages. At any time, many may be in the uninhabited "zero population" phase.

For the larger 2,880-square-mile research area, The Gardens of Kampsville would contribute only 0.0098 person per square mile to the regional density, requiring 10.2 similar villages for a regional density of 0.1 person per square mile or 102 villages for a density of 1 person per square mile.

Adjustments for Missing Burials

The value of 15,557 man-years undoubtedly underestimates the true value for The Gardens of Kampsville mortuary population. Infants are almost certainly underrepresented. (See Chap. 3, Sect. 2.) As noted previously, however, the consequence for population estimation is only a minor loss of man-years. A more significant source of undercounting is the largely undocumented excavation in the Gibson and Pete Klunk mounds prior to the work of Perino and Buikstra.

In 1888, James D. Middleton opened four or five of the Pete Klunk mounds for the Bureau of American Ethnology (Middleton 1888; Thomas 1894:126-128), the results of which are summarized in Table 15. Apparently, only one of these, yielding three burials, was a Middle Woodland mound.

By 1959, Perino (1968:9) notes:

A superficial examination of the structures revealed only that all had been pitted, several seemed to have been seriously damaged, and one [Mound 14, a Late Woodland-Mississippi construction] had been almost completely re-

TABLE 15. *Results of Excavations by James D. Middleton in the Pete Klunk Mound Group, 1888*

Mound no.		Number of burials reported by Middleton	Number of burials excavated by Perino[a]	Remarks
Middleton's sequence	Perino's sequence			
1	14	10	19	Late Woodland-Mississippi mound atop Archaic charnal pit; 9/10 destroyed prior to Perino's excavations.
2	?	0	—	Natural knoll?
5	11?	3	117	Middle Woodland mound.
6	10?	2	7	Late Woodland mound atop Archaic charnal pit.
7	9?	1	2	Late Woodland mound.

Sources: Middleton 1888; Thomas 1894:126-128; Perino 1968.
[a]Counts provided by Jane E. Buikstra (personal communication).

moved for use as fill in a nearby modern cemetery. . . . [However,] in spite of the obvious damage, less than five per cent actual loss in most was noted after excavation, except for Mound 14.

Perino's cross-section drawings suggest that among the Middle Woodland mounds, only Mounds 1, 2, and 5 had suffered major assaults. He observed (1968:12) that

> circular pits each approximately five feet in diameter [had been dug] into Mounds 1, 2, and 5, the excavations penetrating the center of each mound. Since the primary features were in each case off center, little disturbance of them resulted. A few secondary burials only had been destroyed.

Mounds 4 and 5 of the Gibson group were more extensively disturbed. Relic collectors had discovered log tombs in each of these mounds, and a minimum of four (and probably several more) burials were disturbed by them (Perino 1968:119,122; Titterington n.d. [a]).

Even though an objective evaluation of the disturbance in these mound groups is impossible, only a small proportion of all Middle Woodland burials could have been removed. If Perino's estimate of less than 5 percent disturbance of Pete Klunk burials is reliable, then fewer than 19 Middle Woodland burials from that mound group were lost to relic collectors. A total of 30±10 missing Middle Woodland burials from both the Pete Klunk and Gibson groups seems a reasonable conjecture.

The six mounds of the Ben Klunk group present the major gap in the record of The Gardens of Kampsville mortuary population. Though records of early excavations are available, they are brief and uninformative (Middleton 1888; Thomas 1894:128-129). Concerning the Ben Klunk group, Perino (1973a:58) remarks:

> Two small mounds similar to [the Late Woodland Pete Klunk] Mounds 9 and 10 were on the hilltop to the west [of Pete Klunk Mound 14]. On the same hill were two badly pitted Hopewell mounds and another mound somewhat similar to some made by Late Woodland people in the Mississippi period; these were not investigated by this survey.

Perino (personal communication) informs me of the existence of a previously unrecognized sixth mound in the Ben Klunk group (labeled as Mound 3 in Figure 2). On the basis of its location and external morphology, he infers a Late Woodland cultural affiliation. The unnamed mound south of the Ben Klunk group is also a Late Woodland structure according to Perino.

Using his estimate that two of the mounds date to the Middle Woodland period and assuming that they contain burials in a frequency comparable to the other mound groups, one obtains a revised estimate of 641 burials for all three groups. This includes an allowance for 30 missing burials from the Pete Klunk and Gibson groups. Assuming the same mean age at death for the Ben Klunk, Gibson, and Pete Klunk mound groups, an estimated total of 18,709 man-years is obtained for The Gardens of Kampsville mortuary population. A revised table for length of occupation versus village size, based on 641 burials, is given in Table 16.

Number of Habitation Sites

For the adjusted burial population size, Table 17 presents hypothetical regional population levels and their equivalents in multiples of The Gardens of Kampsville's contribution in man-years.

To evaluate Table 17, the total number of Middle Woodland habitation sites in the region is first estimated by projecting the site density, obtained from intensively surveyed sections, to the total research universe. Estimates will be made for three locations:

1. A zone including the western edge of the Illinois Valley and the floodplain adjacent to the river channel.
2. For the eastern valley margin. (A valley margin site is defined as one located either at the bluff base or bluff crest at the edge of the valley or located along a

TABLE 16. *Length of Occupation Versus Population Size of The Gardens of Kampsville, Based on 641 Burials From Three Mound Groups*

Length of occupation (years)	Village size (inhabitants)
1	18,709
5	3,742
10	1,871
25	748
50	374
100	187
150	125
200	94
320	58
550	34
690	27

secondary stream within a mile of its entrance into the Illinois Valley floodplain.)

3. For tributary valleys and adjacent uplands.

The present incomplete survey of habitation sites has documented 32 in location (1), 18 in location (2), and 23 from location (3)—a total of 73 sites (Struever 1968b and personal communication; Farnsworth 1973 and personal communication; Houart 1971 and personal communication).

Documented site locations (shown in Fig. 1) are highly clustered in the Illinois River floodplain and at the edge of the valley, a fact which relates in part to the history of archeological investigations. For locations (1) and (2), the mean north-south distance between clustered habitation sites will be used to estimate the total that would be recorded by a complete survey. In segments of these linear regions where, despite intensive survey, known sites are absent or infrequent, the procedure will be modified by arbitrarily considering the true site frequency as one-half that of the cluster areas. These procedures should provide an estimate of the total number of habitation sites that is somewhat greater than the true value, and it will be appropriate for use in a maximum population estimate.

The clusters defined for location (1) are 1-2-3-4-5; 9-11-13; 27-28-30-31; 35-36-37-38-39-40-41-42-43-44; 45-46; 52-55-57-60; and 77-78-80, the numbering of sites corresponding to that in Figure 1. Mean intracluster spacing of

TABLE 17. *Hypothetical Population Levels for the Lower Illinois Valley, Expressed as Multiples of the Number of Man-Years Lived at The Gardens of Kampsville*

Population size	Population density (per sq mi)		Multiples of man-years lived at The Gardens of Kampsville
	1,000-sq-mi research universe	2,880-sq-mi research universe	
100	0.1	0.035	2.9
288	.29	.1	8.5
576	.58	.2	17
864	.86	.3	25
1,152	1.2	.4	34
1,440	1.4	.5	42
2,160	2.2	.75	63
2,880	2.9	1	85
5,760	5.8	2	169
14,400	14.4	5	423
28,800	28.8	10	847

these sites is 1.08 miles. Regions of known low site density, listed from north to south, lie between Swartz-Florence (#31) and Bixby (#35) sites, between Pulpwood Mill (#44) and Hatcher (#45) sites, between Vaughn (#46) and Newport Landing (#52) sites, and between The Gardens of Kampsville (#60) and DeGerlia Hollow. The combined length of the low-density intervals is 16.6 miles. Thus, for the 67-mile length of the western valley margin and floodplain adjacent to the river channel, the estimated number of sites is

$$\frac{67-16.6}{1.08} + \frac{1}{2}\left(\frac{16.6}{1.08}\right) = 54$$

For location (2), the eastern valley margin, the estimation procedure is complicated by the presence of large secondary valleys having wide mouths in which sites tend to cluster. At the mouths of some of these (specifically Mauvaise Terre and Apple Valleys), the sites are equally oriented in the east-west and north-south direction. To include all such sites in clusters would result in a misleadingly high north-south site density, since an east-west site orientation is characteristic only of junctures of the Illinois Valley with large secondary valleys. I attempted to circumvent this problem by excluding from clusters all sites located essentially east of another site in the mouth of a secondary valley. This step removes Mauvaise Terre-Merriman (#17) site from the Mauvaise Terre cluster and Audrey (#48) site from the Apple Valley cluster. These are added in again later in a special correction for the mouths of large secondary valleys. Next, the clusters for location (2) are defined as 6-8-14-15-16-29; 47-51-54-56-58; and 85-86, the numbering of sites corresponding to that in Figure 1. Mean intracluster spacing of these sites is 1.57 miles. Survey data of the Northwestern University Archeological Program, as well as from Titterington's excavations in western Jersey County (Titterington 1935, n.d. [c]; Shalkop 1949), indicate that the interval between Marquette (#85) and Levis (#58) sites, a distance of 23.2 miles, has a very low frequency of Middle Woodland habitation. Between Apple and Plum creeks, a distance of 20.2 miles, is another low-density interval. Thus,

$$\frac{67-43.4}{1.57} + \frac{1}{2}\left(\frac{43.4}{1.57}\right) = 29 \text{ sites}$$

are predicted for the eastern valley margin, exclusive of eastward-lying sites in the mouths of large secondary valleys. The five large secondary valleys on the east side of the Illinois River are, from north to south, Mauvaise Terre, Sandy, Apple, Macoupin, and Otter. Of these, only the mouth of Sandy Valley lacks intensive survey. Adding in the deleted sites and arbitrarily allotting an "extra" site for Sandy raises the estimated total to 32.

The number of village sites in the secondary valley drainages is difficult to project. Intensive surveys using the "collector-interview" methodology (Farnsworth 1973, Houart 1971) have been conducted for two of the six large tributaries draining the region (Macoupin and Mauvaise Terre); two other large valleys (Apple and Otter) have been partially surveyed. The largest tributary is Macoupin Creek, about 70 miles long and draining one-third of the lower Illinois Valley region. Intensive survey of the Macoupin Valley has yielded only nine Middle Woodland sites (Farnsworth 1973 and personal communication). Mauvaise Terre Creek is much smaller (only 36 miles long); however, there are nine known sites in its valley and on the adjacent bluff crests (Houart 1971 and personal communication). The total for major tributary valleys is 22 sites. In addition, five Middle Woodland sites were discovered (Houart 1971) in an intensive survey of Bay Creek, a 35-mile-long tributary of the Mississippi River—a fact which is mentioned here because of its proximity to the lower Illinois Valley. However, Bay Creek sites are omitted from the estimates that follow.

Partial surveys exist for several small creeks (Crater, Crawford, and Knife), and a thorough survey of small Silver Creek has been accomplished (all four creeks are on the west side of the Illinois River), but no Middle Woodland sites were discovered (Farnsworth personal communication; Houart 1971). The Spring Run site, located along the creek bearing the same name, is the only Middle Woodland site documented thus far on a small tributary of the lower Illinois River.

Except on bluff crests at the margins of river and creek valleys, no upland Middle Woodland sites are known. The dissected uplands lying within 5 miles of the Illinois Valley, which were forested prior to European settlement (Zawacki and Hausfater 1969; Fehrenbacher and Downey 1966), have been surveyed in the 20-mile-long section between Apple and Otter Creeks by means of collector interviews. The same survey method has been used in sections of upland prairie

within the Macoupin Valley drainage. In both instances, results were negative (Farnsworth 1973 and personal communication) and the virtual absence of upland prairie sites is corroborated by survey results for the nearby Sangamon drainage area (Klippel 1971). For purposes of population estimation it seems safe to assume a total absence of upland Middle Woodland villages. Probably there are as yet unrecognized, temporary nonceramic campsites, but it is unnecessary to count these minor, specialized-activity occupations.

To recapitulate, there are 22 documented Middle Woodland sites associated with large tributary valleys of the Illinois Valley, only one from a small tribrurary valley, and none from the upland forest and prairie zones away from the valley margins—for a total of 23 sites outside the main trench of the Illinois Valley. Given the present progress of the survey, a generous estimate would double the presently known number of sites in tributary valley drainages to 46.

A Maximum Estimate

From the preceding results, a total of 54 + 32 + 46 = 132 village sites are predicted for the 2,880-square-mile lower Illinois Valley drainage basin. If all sites were occupied to the same extent as The Gardens of Kampsville (i.e., 18,709 man-years of habitation), regional population density would then be 1.6 individuals per square mile during the Middle Woodland period and regional population size would be 4,500 individuals.

Nine of the 23 documented secondary valley sites are in the smaller 1,000-square-mile research universe, and a reasonably safe upper estimate would be that half of all secondary valley sites are within this smaller region. This leads to an estimated 54 + 32 + 23 = 109 sites in the 1,000-square-mile region. If all sites were occupied to the same extent as The Gardens of Kampsville, population in and adjacent to the Illinois Valley bottomland would have been 3.7 persons per square mile, a total population of 3,700 individuals.

These estimates undoubtedly exceed the actual regional population level by a wide margin. The area of The Gardens of Kampsville, its debris frequency, and the size of its associated burial population all attest to a "quantity of occupation" well above the regional average. Though information about variation in quantity of occupation at Middle Woodland sites is very crude and incomplete, enough exists to form an impression of the consequence of assuming that every site is the equal of The Gardens of Kampsville.

Table 18 presents data on two variables suggestive of the quantity of occupation at lower Illinois Valley Middle Woodland sites:

1. The area-of-scatter of cultural debris on site surfaces.
2. The maximum sherd pick-up rate (per 15 minutes) in timed surface surveys of sites situated in cultivated fields.

The latter variable gives a rough measure of the intensity of occupation as seen from the surface. Maximum, rather than mean, pick-up rates are given because survey conditions at a site may vary from very poor to very good, depending upon the kind of ground cover and degree of rain-wash. Maximum rates obtained under prime survey conditions should be more comparable than rates determined under varying circumstances.

Neither area-of-scatter nor sherd pick-up rate is directly proportional to quantity of occupation. In fact, their product (recorded in Table 18) is a better relative measure of man-years of occupation than the variables themselves. This product ranges between 1 and 1048. The median value of the maximum sherd pick-up rate is 7.5 per 15 mintues, but 15/49 of these rates were less than one-half the median value and 17/49 were more than twice the median. The median area-of-scatter of the 40 sites for which boundaries have been completely determined is 3.0 acres, i.e., less than one-half the minimum area of The Gardens of Kampsville.

These data indicate that a substantial proportion of known sites have a small quantity of occupation. This trend is observable despite a bias toward documentation of richer sites due to the manner in which many were brought to the attention of archeologists. In rich zones of prehistoric occupation such as the bluff base at the edge of the Illinois Valley, any given territory is likely to be hunted by several local collectors. Consequently, tips on the existence of rich sites in such zones filter readily to the archeologist. The locations of small or "unspectacular" sites are not as likely to be commonly known among local collectors, even if such sites are numerous. For example, systematic surveys of sand ridges in the bottoms of the main valley and of secondary valleys have disclosed high densities of sites which are not of special interest to most local collectors and were therefore not previously brought to the attention

of archeologists through desultory local contacts (Struever 1968b, 1968c; Farnsworth 1973).

As systematic survey knowledge increases, this rich site bias will diminish. However, even systematic surface survey favors the discovery of large, rich sites. Large sites are more likely to have part of the ground cover favorable to their discovery; and if buried, they have a higher probability of exposure in gullies, ditches, etc.

The true prehistoric population level therefore must be considerably smaller than the upper limit obtained by the Mound-Village Calibration method because of two factors: (1) Most known sites have a smaller quantity of occupation than The Gardens of Kampsville, and (2) the present site sample overrepresents large sites.

3. PROBLEMS FOR CONTINUING RESEARCH

Both methods of estimating the Middle Woodland population size suggest that the average density in the 2,880-square-mile research area could not have been much greater than one person per square mile. That these semi-independent methods indicate low levels of population lends support to the case. If, on the contrary, the population was much denser than 1 per square mile, then the following corollaries are deducible:

1. Many more large Middle Woodland villages occurred in the region than the presently estimated number.
2. The mortuary population was much larger than estimated for one or more of the following reasons:
   a. Many more mound groups existed than present evidence suggests.
   b. Burial populations for mound groups had a mean size much larger than the present maximum estimates.
   c. A large percentage of Middle Woodland individuals were missing from the mound population because of interment in other locations or destruction of skeletal remains.

More data relevant to these alternatives can, of course, be systematically collected. More indirect information about skeletal destruction will accrue in future work, particularly from the analysis of age-sex distributions of burial populations. However, since the latter alternative can only be excluded through indirect negative evidence, it

TABLE 18. *Area-of-Scatter and Surface Sherd Densities on Middle Woodland Habitation Sites of the Lower Illinois Valley*[a]

Site no.[b]	Site	[A] Area-of-scatter, acres	[B] Maximum number of sherds recovered per 15 min of survey[c]	[A] × [B] Site area × sherd recovery rate
1	Sunset Beach	–	1.5	–
3	Pool	>1.1	58.0	>63
4	Irving	4.6	6.0	28
5	Hinners	3	8.0	24
7	Spring Run	1.4	–	–
8	Marsh	2.5	16.8	42
9	Naples Abbott	6.1	18.3	112
11	Emeline	–	3.0	–
13	Naples Castle	–	18.5	–
14	Bridge	1.7	1.7	3
15	Oxville	–	2.0	–
16	Thomas	1.3	–	–
17	Mauvaise Terre-Merriman	4.1	31.0	127
18	Matthews	>0.6	4.9	>3
19	Calving	>0.2	2.0	>0.4
20	Hubbard	1.9	5.0	10
21	Exeter	2.4	12.3	30
23	Magelitz	1.3	6.0	8
24	Krems	2.7	18.0	49
25	Merritt	1.9	38.3	73
26	Grundy	1.3	2.3	3
27	Ceisler	>2.8	2.3	>6
28	Blue Creek	3.7	7.0	26
29	Plum Creek	7.6	99.0	752
30	Manker-Little League-Monta	–	12.3	–
31	Swartz-Florence	>4.3	9.4	>40
34	Andell-Watt	4.6	16.3	75
35	Bixby	–	5.3	–
37	Ina Knox	>2.8	15.3	>43
40	Buckhorn	3.9	6.2	24
41	Springer	8.5	0.8	7
42	Mound House	10	104.8	1048
46	Vaughn	3	80.0	240
47	Apple Creek	3.5	–	–
48	Audrey	10.1	3.0	30
49	McPherson	3.3	26.5	88
50	Crooked Run	3.6	12.3	44
51	Camerer	4.0	0.3	1
54	Hobson	1.3	7.5	10
55	Kamp	2.2	–	–
56	Bluffdale-Russell	>0.7	7.7	>5
57	Rapp	2.3	2.4	6
63	Titus-Upper Macoupin	5.7	0.3	2
65	Devor	2.3	5.0	12
66	Loy	3.7	3.3	12
67	Edwards	2.8	3.7	10
69	Flautt	1.9	2.0	4
70	Chism	4.7	25.0	118
71	Orange	1.6	8.0	13
72	Spanish Needle	3.1	26.0	81
75	Macoupin	5.8	46.0	267
78	Peisker	2.7	–	–
82	Kiel	>4.4	39.2	>172
86	Duncan Farm	7.5	6.0	45

[a]Based on Struever 1968b, Farnsworth 1973, and unpublished surface survey notes in files of Illinois Valley Archaeological Program; includes virtually all data collected through 1971 survey season.

[b]Refers to numbering of sites on map in Figure 1.

[c]I.e., maximum rate achieved among all timed surface surveys of site.

creates the most serious obstacle to a test of the estimation procedures.

An improved Middle Woodland chronology will reduce a major source of uncertainty in the estimates. This should come as a normal product of continuing archeological research in the region.

Also needed are additional estimates of the mean age of burial populations. Excavation of more burial populations will help achieve a near-zero sample value of r to mitigate the consequences of being unable to calculate a value for growth rate.

Microstyle studies in the lower Illinois Valley and adjacent regions may be useful for defining sociopolitical units and for delineating their boundaries. Population estimates will then become more meaningful than for the present arbitrarily defined research area.

Substantial refinement in the Mound-Village Calibration method is possible. Excavation of the Ben Klunk mound group will reduce the uncertainty in the number of man-years represented by The Gardens of Kampsville. The size and occupational intensity of this habitation site should also receive further investigation. If it could be shown that the frequency of sherds, projectile points, or some other artifact or debris category varies directly with man-years, a more adequate assessment of the number of man-years lived at different sites would then be possible. Calibration of artifact frequencies in terms of man-year equivalents requires joint excavation of mound group/habitation site pairs.

In short, this paper can be regarded as a "work-in-progress" for the investigation of population levels in the lower Illinois Valley. Possibilities for extension and refinement are numerous and can be expected to arise from present and future research conducted in this region.

5

Discussion and Summary

1. COMPARISONS

A better perspective on the low estimate of the Middle Woodland population may be gained by comparing it with native population levels during the early historic period. Estimates of historic tribal densities in eastern North America calculated by James Mooney (published in Kroeber 1939:138-141) are almost uniformly less than one person per square mile. Kroeber observed that in North America, the highest aboriginal densities were usually attained in coastal zones. According to Mooney's estimates, not a single interior group had a density greater than 1 person per square mile. Excluding nonagricultural tribes and various groups of Kroeber's Prairie culture area, the mean population density in eastern North America for the early historic period is calculated as just 0.31 persons per square mile. For the Iliniwek, whose territory included the lower Illinois Valley, Mooney suggested a population of 9,500 persons in a 118,000-square-mile region—a density of 0.080 person per square mile (cf. Temple 1966:11-56). Although this density is very low, it must be noted that the areal base for the density calculation included the drainages of many small rivers and creeks. Since these areas were only marginally exploited during the Middle Woodland period, a Middle Woodland population density computed over the same base would be several times smaller than the maximum of 1 person per square mile suggested for the lower Illinois Valley drainage.

It is questionable whether the low historic Indian densities in eastern North America can be attributed solely to the decimation of populations under the European presence. Historic hunter-gatherer groups of California and the Northwest Coast were considerably more populous than the Eastern Woodland agriculturalists. Kroeber obtained a *mean* density of 1.13 persons per square mile for California, and Mooney's data yield a mean of 0.73 persons per square mile for the Northwest Coast (Kroeber 1939:143). (More recent estimates for California [e.g., Baumhoff

1963] are much higher than Kroeber's.) Even if historic data for the East underestimate population levels just prior to European contact, the continental patterning of estimates suggests that population levels of the interior of eastern North America were relatively low. If this picture is false, it will be necessary to explain why West Coast groups were less affected by European contact than those in the East.

In sum, my estimate of Middle Woodland population levels is roughly comparable to levels suggested for eastern North America during the early historic period.

It is a common opinion that the evidence for complex Hopewellian societies in the eastern United States requires a concomitant high population density. However, some rather complex societies persisted during the historic period with rather low population levels. For example, the highly stratified societies of the historic Natchez, Avoyel, and Taensa consisted of 5,300 individuals in a combined territory of 11,000 square miles—a density of 0.49 person per square mile (Kroeber 1939:139).

In part the low prehistoric population level estimated in this study is a consequence of the choice of regional boundaries. Probably a better unit for comparison would include both the lower Illinois Valley and adjacent Mississippi Valley, since their proximity and cultural similarity suggest that they were embraced by a single sociopolitical entity. Because of the concentration of human populations around the food resources of the rivers, backwater lakes, and forests in and adjacent to main valleys (Struever 1964, 1968c; Parmalee, Paloumpis, and Wilson 1972; Hill 1970; Asch, Ford, and Asch 1972), the effect of adjacent, parallel major river valleys would probably be to double the size of population in a region redefined to encompass both valleys. Potential for social interaction also would have been greater for a population concentrated along linear zones rather than for one uniformly dispersed throughout the region. Perhaps population size and density within the two-valley system was thus sufficient to support social organization of the complexity postulated for Illinois Hopewell by some archeologists (Deuel 1952; Wray and MacNeish 1961).

An alternative viewpoint (mentioned in Chap. 4, Sect. 1) is that in Illinois the evidence for Middle Woodland social stratification, craft specialization, economic surpluses, trade in luxury items, labor commitment to mound-building, agriculture, and other attributes of complex societies is modest and has sometimes been emphasized too vigorously.

The comparison with historic population levels has not cast doubt upon the validity of my Middle Woodland estimate. However, the comparison is not entirely satisfying. This is partly due to uncertainties about the disruptive effects of the European presence and also to the questionable reliability of the historic data. (Estimates of native populations north of Mexico range from a low of 1 million [Kroeber 1939] to a high of 10 to 12 million [Dobyns 1966].) Fundamentally, however, such comparisons are unsatisfactory because of the deficiency of theory relating *absolute* population size and density to social and ecological variables.

2. SUMMARY

The major aim of this paper was to estimate the size and density of the Middle Woodland population of the lower Illinois Valley region. This I accomplished by dividing measures of the man-years of occupation in the region by the length of the Middle Woodland period.

A major problem for estimates based on man-years has been that this variable confounds population size and length of occupation. For community-level estimates, the duration of occupation of a prehistoric settlement or of use of a cemetery is usually as difficult to ascertain as population size itself. Consequently, a regional approach was employed and a timespan chosen which was long enough to achieve substantial reduction in the relative error in dating it.

In developing the estimates, it was necessary to explore demographic characteristics of the Gibson-Klunk burial population, consisting of 533 individuals. Attention was first directed to the demographic model, which specifies the interrelations of vital statistics. In order to compute vital statistics from age-sex characteristics of a burial population, certain restrictive assumptions were

required, chief among them being (1) that age-structure of the prehistoric population was stable through time, (2) that the growth rate r has a specific value (which cannot be measured empirically), and (3) that if migration occurred, the population age structure remained unaltered. The illustrative calculation of several vital statistics and a discussion of assumptions upon which they are based developed into a secondary focus of the paper.

The number of man-years lived by the Gibson-Klunk population and the mean age at death were calculated for use in the population estimates. The Gibson-Klunk age-sex structure was also examined for possible biases indicating incomplete representation of the entire mortuary population in mounds. Comparisons with other pre-Modern burial populations and with twentieth century populations suffering high mortality rates suggested that the Gibson-Klunk age-sex structure was biased only with respect to the underrepresentation of infants. Missing infants do not create a serious problem for purposes of population estimation because they contribute little to the cumulative man-years lived by a population.

The choice of a value for growth rate r was an important concern of the study because of its strong consequences for the computed values of prehistoric vital statistics. It was shown that for a timespan as long as the Middle Woodland period the mean value of r must be near zero.

One estimation method was based on a partial census of Middle Woodland mound burials in the lower Illinois Valley, from which population size was estimated by the formula:

$$\text{Mean population} \doteq \frac{M\overline{N}\overline{A}}{L}$$

where M = number of Middle Woodland mound groups in the region, maximally estimated as 160 groups; $\overline{N}$ = mean number of burials in a mound group maximally estimated as 390 individuals; $\overline{A}$ = mean age at death in the burial population, estimated as 29 years from the Gibson-Klunk skeletal series; and L = length of the Middle Woodland occupation, 550 years. Determining reasonable ranges for these variables was a major task. In addition, the formula makes two major assumptions that required justification: (1) that most of the Middle Woodland deceased were interred in mound cemeteries; (2) that the total number of deceased times the mean age at death in the mortuary population gives the required measure of man-years. The maximum estimate of population density obtained by this method was approximately 1 person per square mile in the lower Illinois Valley drainage basin—i.e., less than 3,000 individuals.

The second method obtained a maximum estimate of man-years lived in the region from data on the number of habitation sites times the number of man-years lived at The Gardens of Kampsville site. Since The Gardens of Kampsville is larger and was more intensively occupied than most sites, the number of man-years lived there (estimated as 18,709 from the Gibson-Klunk mortuary population) was used as an upper bound for the mean among all sites in the region. Using this figure in conjunction with an estimate of 132 Middle Woodland habitation sites, an upper limit of 1.6 persons per square mile was obtained for population density in the lower Illinois Valley drainage basin. There are reasons for believing that the method overestimated the actual population density by a substantial margin.

In a scientific estimate of numerical parameters, error evaluation is of equal importance to the estimated parameters. For prehistoric population estimates, problems of bias caused by missing data and nonrepresentative samples are greater than the uncertainties of sampling error. Consequently, the reliability of an estimate cannot be summed up adequately by computing its error variance. None-theless, even when biases are considerable, one can often ascertain a reasonable range for a variable; and the construction of upper and lower bounds for population levels, rather than a point estimate, was one response of this study to the challenge of bias. A few assumptions in the argument could not be justified to the complete satisfaction of the author, and these were explicitly noted.

Insofar as possible, the population estimates were obtained without dependence upon social and ecological assumptions about Middle Woodland peoples and their environments. Consequently, for most problems requiring information about population levels, these estimates can be used without introducing circularity into the reasoning.

In conclusion, the long-range commitment of the Northwestern University Archeological Program to research in the Illinois Valley is founded upon the premise that intensive regional programs are an important means of probing more deeply into processes of prehistoric culture change—that the accumulation of archeological knowledge about a region leads not to attenuation in the returns of further research but rather to an expansion in the capacity for recognizing and solving processual problems. This paper is a portion of that work; its value depends largely upon its articulation within the greater context of lower Illinois Valley research.

Appendix A
A Naïve Exposition of Integral Notation

For readers not acquainted with calculus, the following exposition of integral notation may make the sections on vital statistics more intelligible. One may think of the expression

$$\int_a^\beta k(a)\,da \qquad (A-1)$$

as consisting of two directions: first, to plot the values of the variable $k(a)$ (the vertical coordinate of the graph in Fig. 3 of the text) against the values of a (the horizontal coordinate); second, to calculate the area of the shaded region in Figure 3 that lies beneath the resulting curve and above the a-axis and which is bounded on the left and right by a-values of a and β.

Divide the interval between a and β into n equal parts of width Δa. In the figure, it is obvious that the product

$$k(a) \cdot \Delta a$$

gives the area of a rectangle that has *approximately* the same area as the region beneath the curve and between $a = a$ and $a = a + \Delta a$. The total area of the shaded region is approximately the sum of areas of n successive rectangles:

$$k(a) \cdot \Delta a + k(a+\Delta a) \cdot \Delta a + k(a+2\Delta a) \cdot \Delta a + \ldots$$

$$+ k(a + (n-1)\Delta a) \cdot \Delta a = \sum_{j=0}^{n-1} k(a+i\Delta a) \cdot \Delta a$$

The larger the number of subdivisions n (i.e., the thinner the rectangles), the closer the approximation will be. Indeed, the approximation can be made as accurate as desired by indefinitely decreasing the width Δa of the rectangles. In the limiting case of "infinitesimally small width," the symbol Δa is replaced by da (a single symbol meaning "infinitesimally small interval" of a, *not* "d times a"). Thus, the area of the "infinitesimally thin rectangle" at a value a along the abscissa is represented as $k(a)\,da$, and the summation of the "infinitesimally small areas" between a and β is indicated by the notation in expression (A-1).

Also in the text, the double integral notation, e.g.,

$$\int_a^\beta \int_r^s d(a, t)\,dt\,da$$

will be encountered. Three-dimensional coordinates are required to specify the joint values of a, t, and $d(a, t)$. The variable $d(a, t)$ maps a curved surface above the at-plane for specified values of a and t. The double integral represents the volume of the solid which is bounded by this surface and the at-plane, by values of t which are limited to the interval (r, s), and by a-values limited to the interval (a, β).

Appendix B
Proofs Relating to
Calculation of Vital Statistics

Four statements are to be proved for all values of r in stable populations.

1. *Statement*: The age distribution of the *burial* population is stable; i.e., among all deaths, the proportion of deaths that occur within any age group over a period of time s is constant for any value of s. Furthermore, the proportion is independent of the absolute size of the living population.

Proof: Suppose that a burial population accumulates between time $t = 0$ and $t = s$. Then the total number of deaths during this time, within the age interval (a, β), is represented by

$$_{\beta-a}D_a = \int_a^\beta \int_0^s d(a, t) \, dt \, da$$

The number of deaths at a specific age depends on the size of the age class and its mortality rate, i.e.,

$$d(a, t) \, dt \, da = k(a, t)\mu(a) \, dt \, da \qquad (B-1)$$

Individuals of age a at time t are members of the cohort born at time $t-a$. Thus,

$$k(a, t) \, dt \, da = k(0, t-a)p(a) \, dt \, da \qquad (B-2)$$

Also, in a stable population, the size of any age class is governed by the exponential growth function, just as the total population size is, so that

$$k(0, t-a) \, dt \, da = k(0,0)e^{r(t-a)} \, dt \, da \qquad (B-3)$$

Substitution of Equations (B-3) and (B-2) into (B-1) gives

$$d(a,t) \, dt \, da = k(0,0)e^{r(t-a)}p(a)\mu(a) \, dt \, da \qquad (B-4)$$

so that the total number of deaths in the age interval (a, β) is

$$_{\beta-a}D_a = \int_a^\beta \int_0^s d(a, t) \, dt \, da$$
$$= \int_a^\beta \int_0^s k(0,0)e^{r(t-a)}p(a)\mu(a) \, dt \, da$$
$$= k(0,0) \int_0^s e^{rt} \, dt \int_a^\beta e^{-ra}p(a)\mu(a) \, da$$

Similarly, the total burial population size D is

$$D = \int_0^\omega \int_0^s d(a,t) \, dt \, da = \int_0^\omega \int_0^s k(a,t)\mu(a) \, dt \, da$$
$$= k(0,0) \int_0^s e^{rt} \, dt \int_0^\omega e^{-ra}p(a)\mu(a) \, da \qquad (B-5)$$

Thus, the proportion of the burial population between ages a and β is

$$\frac{_{\beta-a}D_a}{D} = \frac{\int_a^\beta \int_0^s d(a,t) \, da \, dt}{\int_0^\omega \int_0^s d(a,t) \, da \, dt} = \frac{\int_a^\beta e^{-ra}p(a)\mu(a) \, da}{\int_0^\omega e^{-ra}p(a)\mu(a) \, da}$$

This demonstrates that the proportion of individuals in a burial population who are at a given age is independent both of time and absolute population size.

Comments: All the vital statistics calculated in this paper—with the exception of man-years and population size—can be obtained from the proportional distribution of ages in the burial population. Neither population size, period of accumulation for the burials, nor time in any other sense, is essential to the computations, which are simplified by proceeding as if all burials had been produced simultaneously—that is to say, during the interval $(t, t + dt)$.

2. *Statement*: If

$$l(0) = \int_a^\omega e^{rx}D(x) \, dx$$

as defined in Equation (3-17) and p. 36, the values of $l(a)$ are given by

$$l(a) = \int_a^\omega e^{rx}D(x) \, dx$$

Proof: The $D(x) \, dx$ burials in the age class $(x, x + dx)$ accumulated over a period of time s. Hence,

$$D(x) \, dx = [\int_0^s d(x,t) \, dt] \, dx$$

and $l(0)$ can be rewritten as

$$l(0) = \int_0^\omega e^{rx} [\int_0^s d(x,t) \, dt] \, dx$$

From the relationships developed in Statement 1, Equation (B-4), it follows that

$$l(0) = \int_0^\omega e^{rx} [\int_0^s d(x,t) \, dt] \, dx$$
$$= \int_0^s k(0,0)e^{rt} [\int_0^\omega p(x)\mu(x) \, dx] \, dt$$

By the definition of mortality rate,

$$p(x)\mu(x) = -\frac{dp(x)}{dx}$$

Thus,

$$l(0) = \int_0^s k(0,0)e^{rt} \left[\int_0^\omega \left(-\frac{dp(x)}{dx} \right) dx \right] dt$$

$$= \int_0^s k(0,0)e^{rt} \left[-p(x)|_0^\omega \right] dt$$

$$= \int_0^s k(0,0)e^{rt}(1) dt$$

Now return to the value of $l(a)$:

$$l(a) = p(a)l(0) = \int_0^s k(0,0)e^{rt}p(a) dt \quad \text{(B-6)}$$

Noting that

$$p(a) = \int_a^\omega \left(-\frac{dp(x)}{dx} \right) dx$$

we have

$$l(a) = \int_0^s k(0,0)e^{rt} \left[\int_a^\omega p(x)\mu(x) dx \right] dt$$

$$= \int_a^\omega \int_0^s k(0,0)e^{rt}p(x)\mu(x) dt dx$$

Using Equation (B-4), Statement 1, the following result is obtained:

$$l(a) = \int_a^\omega e^{rx} \left[\int_0^s d(x,t) dt \right] dx = \int_a^\omega e^{rx}D(x) dx$$

This is the required relationship.

Comments: The relationship between the age-specific mortality in a burial population and the history of death in the hypothetical cohort is a simple corollary of this proof. Consider the number of deaths occurring between ages a and β in the cohort. Using elementary rules of integration, this number is represented as

$$l(a)-l(\beta) = \int_a^\omega e^{rx}\int_0^s d(x,t)dt dx - \int_\beta^\omega e^{rx}\int_0^s d(x,t)dt dx$$

$$= \int_a^\beta e^{rx}\int_0^s d(x,t) dt dx$$

For a small age interval, the value of e^{rx} will not vary widely and may conveniently be considered a constant with value $e^{r(a+\beta)/2}$. Then

$$l(a)-l(\beta) \doteq e^{r(a+\beta)/2} \int_a^\beta \int_0^s d(x,t)dt dx \quad \text{(B-7)}$$

that is, the number of deaths in the cohort during the given age interval is *approximately* directly proportional to the number of individuals at the same age in the burial population.

For stable, stationary populations, e^{rx} *is* a constant (=1). Then Equation (B-7) is exact and the death history in the cohort exactly duplicates the age structure of death in the burial population.

3. *Statement*: The total size of the mortuary population D divided by the crude death rate d gives the number of man-years lived by the population during the period of time that the burials accumulated.

Proof: The number of man-years lived by the community between initiation of occupation at $t = 0$ and termination at $t = s$ is represented by

$$\text{Man-years} = \int_0^s \int_0^\omega k(a,t) da dt$$

Even though the length of occupation s is unknown, it can be shown that D/d must equal this integral. In Statement 1, Equation (B-5), it was indicated that

$$D = \int_0^\omega \int_0^s k(a,t)\mu(a) dt da \quad \text{(B-8)}$$

At time t, the crude death rate is represented as

$$d = \frac{\int_0^\omega k(a,t)\mu(a) da}{\int_0^\omega k(a,t) da} \quad \text{(B-9)}$$

Because d is time-independent, it is possible to integrate the numerator and denominator of Equation (B-9) over the length of occupation without changing the value of the fraction:

$$d = \frac{\int_0^s \int_0^\omega k(a,t)\mu(a) da dt}{\int_0^s \int_0^\omega k(a,t) da dt} \quad \text{(B-10)}$$

Dividing Equation (B-8) by (B-10) gives

$$\frac{D}{d} = \int_0^s \int_0^\omega k(a,t) da dt$$

as required.

4. *Statement*: The number of man-years lived by the population contemporary with the accumulating burial population may also be expressed as

$$\int_0^\omega e^{-ra}l(a) da$$

where the initial size $l(0)$ of the hypothetical cohort is fixed according to the procedures of p. 36.

Proof: Start by using the expression for $l(a)$ indicated by Equation (B-6):

$$l(a) = \int_0^s k(0,0)e^{rt}p(a) dt$$

Then:

$$\int_0^\omega e^{-ra}l(a) da = \int_0^\omega \int_0^s e^{r(t-a)}k(0,0)p(a) dt da$$

and using Equations (B-2) and (B-3), this becomes:

$$\int_0^\omega e^{-ra}l(a) da = \int_0^\omega \int_0^s k(a,t) dt da$$

that is,

$$\int_0^\omega e^{-ra}l(a) da = D/d$$

Appendix C
Documentation for
Middle Woodland Cremation

Baehr Mound Group (Snyder 1894, 1895a, 1895b, 1898)

John F. Snyder excavated three mounds of the Baehr group during the 1890's. Ashes in the fill of Mounds 2 and 4 probably relate to the mounds being constructed with earth from a habitation area. Mound 2 was erected over an area of burned soil covered by a sand floor, but no human skeletal remains—either burned or unburned—were observed at the base of the mound.

In the only other mound investigated by Snyder (Mound 1), the evidence for cremation was unmistakable (Snyder 1895a:79):

> The initial step in rearing this stupendous monument . . . was laying down on the alluvial soil an oval-shaped layer of clay, ten feet in width by eighteen feet in length, and less than a foot in thickness. Over this, and extending beyond the limits of our excavation, the surface had been covered with sand, and the whole area burnt by a long continued fire, in which many human bones were incinerated. . . . [Next a] deposit of 6,199 flints was covered with a stratum of clay, 10 inches in thickness; and on this another fire had been maintained for some time, in which a few bodies, or skeletons, had been cremated. Associated with these charred remains were found [many artifacts] but all more or less destroyed by fire and natural decay.

A minimum number of individuals cremated in Mound 1 cannot be determined from Snyder's reports.

Bedford Mound Group (Perino n.d.[a]; Struever 1960:184-193)

Four of the seven mounds investigated by Gregory Perino were lacking in evidence for cremation and apparently for any use of fire as well. Lenses of charcoal were found near several inclusive burials placed in the superstructure of Mound 4, but these were not linked to cremation activities. In Mound 8, a child burned in the pelvic region was discovered; the charring did not take place at the site of burial. The log tomb situated between Mounds 10 and 11 had been burned, and a portion of a charred skull and a few unburned vertebrae were found within the feature.

Duncan Farm Mound Group (McAdams 1881:711-712; Mohrman and Blake n.d.)

McAdams reported a baked clay basin containing dry ashes in the mound excavated by him, but no cremated bone was mentioned. From the southfacing bluff at the site, Mohrman and Blake reported several cremated burials and/or a crematorium which had been disturbed by bulldozing. However, these were not in a definite mound context, nor was their cultural affiliation determined.

Gibson Mound Group (Buikstra 1972)

The central feature of Mound 6 contained burned fragmentary remains of a single individual who had not been cremated at the mound site. The other mounds yielded no additional evidence for cremation.

Hardin Mound Group (Middleton 1888; Thomas 1889, 1894:130-131)

Excavating in Mound 1 in 1888, James Middleton discovered a small layer of burned earth about 8 inches thick and 7 feet below the mound surface in its northeast quadrant. The layer contained dispersed charcoal but no ash, and Middleton concluded that it was not an *in situ* deposit. Four small fire beds were found, two of them on a layer of stone capping the primary mound. The only direct evidence for cremation was provided by a small deposit of burned bones resting on the original ground surface. The cremation had occurred elsewhere.

Hazelherst Mound Group (Fecht 1955:29-30; Perino n.d.[b]).

For Mound 8, of indeterminate cultural affiliation, Fecht reported the discovery of "five extended burials, resting upon a pile of burned wood ashes," but cremation was not implied. Perino believes that the ashy substance is niter, not ash.

Hilderbrand Mound (Griffin and Morgan 1941:28)

"Ash beds" discovered in the Hilderbrand mound (Meredosia-Hilderbrand mound group) probably derive from the habitation site midden which was used as mound fill.

Kamp Mound Group (Griffin and Morgan 1941:35-39; Struever 1960)

Evidence for fire or cremation was observed in three of the four excavated mounds. Lower leg bones of one skeleton in Mound 2 were badly charred. Though Taylor noted no associated charcoal or ashes (Griffin and Morgan 1941), Struever (1960:117) suggests that "fire in close proximity, but not cremation itself" may have been a part of the mortuary ceremony resulting in the incomplete charring of this skeleton. Beneath a stone slab "pavement" in Mound 4 were found two piles of burned and unburned human bones—the only osteological remains discovered in the mound. Two or more adults were represented in one pile and an unstated number in the other. No evidence for *in situ* fires was noted for Mound 4, and thus, the charred bones were probably deposited from cremation fires located elsewhere.

In Mound 9, much ceremonial activity involving fire was adduced. However, though *in situ* fires antedated and coincided with some of the burial activity, no cremated bone was found. Struever (1960:90) interpreted a fire-hardened crust of ash, burnt clay, and sand covering part of the burial crypt as a result of repeated episodes of burning followed by careful removal of the burned material. Thus, if cremation occurred, the osteological evidence for it must have been removed along with the remains of the fire.

Pete Klunk Mound Group (Perino 1968:9-124)

Eight Middle Woodland mounds in this group were excavated completely. Two of them (Mounds 1 and 2) revealed no evidence of cremation or other activities involving fire, though beneath Mound 1 a burned tree stump yielded enough charcoal for dating. Intrusive, charred Late Woodland skeletal remains were encountered in Mound 6, but the mound produced no Middle Woodland cremations. Below Mound 7 and in the mound's lower level, quantities of burned soil and limestone, charcoal, and charred bone were observed

and were attributed solely to the Archaic component of the mound. An "ash pit" lay at the base of the secondary cap of Mound 13, but the pit contained Late Woodland sherds.

In three mounds, cremation and/or other activities involving fire occurred in definite Middle Woodland context. "A small handful of charred human bone fragments" constituted the only contents of a large subfloor tomb in Mound 12 (Perino 1968:114). No other human bone occurred in the mound nor was there evidence of *in situ* burning.

Mound 5, with 36 Middle Woodland burials, produced one instance of charred bone—the top of the cranium and a portion of one arm of an articulated child. No cremation fire was associated.

Three areas of burning were discovered in Mound 11, which contained approximately 120 Middle Woodland burials. One of them is described as follows (Perino 1968:100):

Burials 92, 93—The articulated skeletons of an adolescent thirteen years of age and a male fifty-three years of age which had been buried one over the other in a twelve-inch-deep grave located beneath the east side of the primary mound.... It had been used as a crematory, the male skeleton having been placed face down and fire burned over him which charred the upper surface of the bones, especially those of the lower extremities. Afterwards, four inches of soil was placed on the remains and Burial 92 was interred in a semi-flexed position head to feet reversed. Next, the grave was filled to original ground level and then a fire reddening an area of six feet in diameter and to a depth of six inches was built over the grave. Large limestone slabs were then placed on the fired area.

Elsewhere in Mound 11, outside the primary mound and on the original ground surface, was a heavily fired area three feet in diameter from which charcoal but no charred bone was noted.

A third instance of burning is tersely described by Perino (1968:96): In excavating Tomb B into the subsoil, it became evident that "the Hopewellians had gone through some fire-reddened soil marking the eastern edge of a crematory made from a grave pit, and particles of the fired clay were found in the tomb fill." Evidence that this pit served specifically as a crematory is not given, nor is it clear that its association was with Middle Woodland mortuary activities rather than with the Archaic component of the mound group.

In addition, some bones of Burial 6, an extended adult skeleton inclusive in the secondary mound, were burned (Jane Buikstra, personal communication).

In summary, three of eight Middle Woodland mounds (Mounds 5, 11, and 12) yielded burned Middle Woodland skeletal material, involving about 4 individuals in a burial population of more than 370. Only the cremation in Mound 12 had proceeded far enough to reduce the skeleton to fragments.

Knight Mound Group (Griffin et al. 1970)

Only two instances of activities involving the use of fire were reported for eight excavated Middle Woodland mounds. At the periphery of Mound 16 were found the fragmentary bones of an adult male and a child, underlain by a charcoal layer 3½ feet in diameter. If any of the bone was cremated, it was not so reported. Mound 4 contained a fire pit covered by limestone slabs. Ash (or possibly niter) covered the floor of the pit and also occurred in a thin layer on and around the stones.

Meppen Mound Group (Fecht 1955:32)

A cremated burial in an undetermined cultural context was discovered in Mound 1, which contained both Middle Woodland and Middle Mississippi burials.

Merrigan Mound Group (Struever 1970; Wadlow and LaDassor 1951; McAdams 1884)

McAdams excavated the largest mound of this group, discovering a large, shallow basin with a clay floor which, according to the excavator, was "made hard, perhaps by fire" (Struever 1970:50). In their reexamination of the central basin in 1950, Wadlow and LaDassor reported that the light clay subsoil on the floor of the basin had been leveled and tamped, but they did not suggest that it was fire-hardened. McAdams noted ashes at the edges of the basin, and Wadlow and LaDassor also observed ash layers atop the primary and secondary mounds, which were covered by a huge tertiary mound cap. The possibility that the excavators mistook niter for ash cannot be excluded. In any event, the mound revealed no direct evidence for cremation.

Montezuma Mound Group (Fowke 1905; Perino n.d.[a]; Struever 1960:193-194)

The 1905 excavations in Mounds 1 to 8 produced no documentation for cremation prac-

tices. Ashes and charcoal occurred intermittently throughout the fill of Mound 1, but this probably reflects the use of midden from a habitation area as the mound fill. When Mound 1 was about 2½ feet high, a pit 16 inches in diameter was excavated, and in it a fire was built. Apparently, it was unconnected with cremation practices.

Three of the six remaining mounds, which were investigated by Gregory Perino, produced no evidence for fire or cremation. The log tomb of Mound 9 had been burned, and it contained disturbed, burned bones. On the original ground surface of Mound 14 lay an in situ cremation consisting of small bits of charred bone and charcoal. Soil beneath the cremation area was burned to a depth of 4 inches. Nearby on a raised earth platform was a small pile of charred bone fragments and two fire-damaged Snyders projectile points. The central tomb of Mound 15 had also been burned, and inside it were charred bones from a human foot.

Pilot's Peak Mound Group (Perino n.d.[a]; Struever 1960:195)

Bones, some of which were charred, were scattered about the floor of a log tomb, in Mound 1. Perino interpreted the fire-blackened and irregular base of the tomb as a consequence of brush-burning prior to erection of the mound. The only other excavated mound (Mound 3) gave no evidence for cremation.

Robertson Mound Group (Griffin and Morgan 1941:33-34)

The cultural affiliation of the Robertson group, consisting of two mounds, is unknown. This is particularly unfortunate because in the lower Illinois Valley region it is the one mound group of possible Middle Woodland origin where extensive cremation reminiscent of Ohio Hopewell occurred. J. L. B. Taylor excavated the mounds during the 1920's. His methods and his reporting do not permit estimates of the amount of burned bone or the number of individuals represented.

Three burned clay areas were discovered in Mound 1. One of them, situated 30 feet from the center of the mound, was 16 feet long, 4 feet wide, and 3 to 4 inches thick. Clay had been placed in a trench at the original ground surface and then burned to the consistency of brick. A smaller burned clay basin was superimposed over this one, and between the two basins was a "2-inch bed of loose earth, ashes, and bits of burned clay in which was found numerous fragments of burned bone" (Griffin and Morgan 1941:33). Taylor specifically noted a total absence of charcoal from the first burned clay area.

A second burned clay "altar" 8 feet long, 4 feet wide, and thicker than the first was discovered nearby. "It also had the full length of the basin filled with burned bones, but in addition a considerable amount of charcoal was present" (Griffin and Morgan 1941:33).

A third crematory basin 3 feet wide and 4 feet long "carried the usual amount of burned bone but very little charcoal" (Griffin and Morgan 1941:33-34).

In testing Mound 2, Taylor discovered another small area of burned clay which he did not excavate, however.

Appendix D
Documentation for Middle Woodland Mound Groups

Baehr Mound Group

| Mound no. | Dimensions (ft) | | | Minimum number of individuals | | Cultural affiliation | Excavation techniques |
	L	W	H	Middle Woodland	Total		
1	180	100	30	7	9	Middle Woodland + intrusive burials of unknown affiliation.	14-ft-wide center shaft + two 20-ft-wide cross-trenches; about ½ excavated.
2	165	82	24	5	6	Middle Woodland + intrusive burial of unknown affiliation.	20-ft-wide trench running transversely through center of mound, partially removed by plow and scraper.
3	96	96	15	—	—	—	Not excavated.
4	33	33	6	2	4	Middle Woodland + intrusive (?) burials of unknown affiliation.	Almost entirely removed.
A[a]	98	98	8	—	—	Probably Mississippi.	Not excavated.

Notes: Located on the Illinois River floodplain about ½ mile west of the present river channel opposite Indian Creek and less than 5 miles north of the lower Illinois Valley research universe, in Brown County. Excavated by John F. Snyder in the 1890's.

Sources: Snyder 1894, 1895a, 1895b, 1898; Griffin 1941; Thomas 1894:120.

[a]Platform mound.

Bedford Mound Group

| Mound no. | Dimensions (ft) | | | Minimum number of individuals | | Cultural affiliation | Excavation techniques |
	L	W	H	Middle Woodland	Total		
1	30	30	6	5	5	Middle Woodland.	Mound largely excavated prior to Perino's work; burials were disturbed.
2	—	—	—	—	—	—	Previously excavated.
3	70	50	10-12	—	—	—	Previously excavated.
4	45	45	8½	30	30	Middle Woodland; C-14 date of A.D. 230±125 (M-445) from carbonized grass or mat beneath Burial 19, 6 inches beneath mound surface; no diagnostic cultural items associated with burials.	Had been pitted 3 times prior to Perino's work.

Bedford Mound Group (Cont.).

Mound no.	Dimensions (ft)			Minimum number of individuals		Cultural affiliation	Excavation techniques
	L	W	H	Middle Woodland	Total		
5	~20	~20	4	–	–	–	Previously disturbed.
6	10	10	3	–	–	–	Previously disturbed.
7	~20	~20	3	–	–	–	Previously disturbed.
8	90	60	10	13	13	Middle Woodland.	–
9	56	56	10	3	3	Middle Woodland; C-14 date of A.D. 400±125 (M-446) from log of central tomb containing diagnostic Hopewell artifacts.	–
10-11	220	Biconical 64	12½	10	10	Middle Woodland; C-14 dates of A.D. 20±125 (M-443) and A.D. 10± 125 (M-444) obtained, respectively, from charcoal in crematory basin between the mounds and from charred timbers of log tomb between mounds.	–
12	80-90	80-90	20	21	22	Middle Woodland + later(?) flexed intrusive burial.	Had been badly disturbed prior to Perino's work.
13	30	30	3	0	10	Late Woodland.	Burials were occasionally exposed by plowing prior to Perino's investigations.
14	15	15	3	–	–	Perino judges mound to be of Late Woodland origin.	Not excavated.
15	Nearly the same dimensions as no. 14 but a little higher.			–	–	Perino judges mound to be of Late Woodland origin.	Not excavated.
16	40	40	3½	0	23	Late Woodland.	About 1/3 excavated.

Notes: Located on western bluff crest at Illinois Valley margin, in Pike County. Excavated by Gregory Perino, 1955-1956. In general, mounds were incompletely excavated, with emphasis upon obtaining central burials; there was no systematic search for subfloor burials. Evaluation of skeletal series by J. Buikstra augmented some of the burial counts appearing in Perino's field report.

Sources: Pernio n.d.[a]; Buikstra 1972; Crane and Griffin 1958b, 1959; Struever 1960:184-192, 1968b:246-247.

Brangenberg Mound Group

Mound no.	Dimensions (ft)			Minimum number of individuals		Cultural affiliation	Excavation techniques
	L	W	H	Middle Woodland	Total		
1[a]	9	5	≤2	7	7	Middle Woodland.	–
2[a]	12.6	7	–	10	10	Middle Woodland.	–
3[b]	–	–	–	5	5	Middle Woodland.	–

Notes: Located on western bluff crest at Illinois Valley margin, in Calhoun County. Excavated in 1928 by J. L. B. Taylor, probably completely. "Mounds" were little more than stone graves. Published field report is vague concerning exact number of individuals discovered.

Source: Griffin and Morgan 1941:39-44.

[a] Rectangular stone slab grave.

[b] Roughly rectangular stone graves.

Tom Collins (Gallinipper) Mound Group

Mound no.	Dimensions (ft)			Minimum number of individuals		Cultural affiliation	Excavation techniques
	L	W	H	Middle Woodland	Total		
1	–	–	–	16	16	Middle Woodland.	Artifacts and skeletal remains recovered by T. Collins in wake of destruction by bulldozer.
2	–	–	–	–	–	Mississippi(?).	–

Note: Located in floodplain of Illinois Valley adjacent to west side of present river channel, in Calhoun County.
Sources: Struever 1968b:267-268; Thompson 1968; Buikstra 1972.

Duncan Farm Mound Group

Mound no.	Dimensions (ft)			Minimum number of individuals		Cultural affiliation	Excavation techniques
	L	W	H	Middle Woodland	Total		
No number[a]	100	15?	16	5	5	Middle Woodland.	Partially excavated with plough and road scrapers.
No number[b]	–	–	–	0	0	Middle Woodland.	Excavator and excavation techniques unknown.

Notes: Located in bottoms and on adjacent ridge crest north of the Illinois River, in southern Jersey County. The mound excavated by McAdams was said to be one of a dozen on top of the ridge; a large loaf-shaped mound in the bottoms was mentioned also (McAdams 1881:711). Titterington indicated existence of two bottomland mounds and several smaller mounds on the south-sloping bluff—one of the latter yielding Hopewell artifacts. More recently, Mohrman and Blake mentioned one mound in the bottoms and one small mound on a bluff and reported finding several Hopewell interaction sphere items from a bulldozer-disturbed area of the ridge (from subfloor pits of leveled mounds?).
Sources: McAdams 1881:711-712; Mohrman and Blake n.d.; Titterington 1935:6-7; Struever 1968b:280-281; Rinaldo 1937.
[a]Excavated by McAdams (1881).
[b]One of the smaller mounds on the south-sloping bluff reported by Titterington (1935).

Gibson Mound Group

Mound no.	Dimensions (ft)			Minimum number of individuals		Cultural affiliation	Excavation techniques
	L	W	H	Middle Woodland	Total		
1	50	44	4½	21	21	Middle Woodland.	Completely excavated.
2	60	34	5	60	60	Middle Woodland.	Completely excavated.
3	47	35	3½	28	28	Middle Woodland.	Completely excavated.
4	100	100	11	7	7	Middle Woodland.	Trenched by L. Gibson, who excavated tomb(s); mound removal completed by Perino/Buikstra.
5	65	53	4½	35	35	Middle Woodland.	Trenched by L. Gibson, who excavated tomb(s); mound removal completed by Perino/Buikstra.

Gibson Mound Group (Cont.).

Mound no.	Dimensions (ft)			Minimum number of individuals		Cultural affiliation	Excavation techniques
	L	W	H	Middle Woodland	Total		
6	50	46	6	2	2	Middle Woodland.	Completely excavated.
7	30	28	2-3	0	2	Late Woodland.	Completely excavated.
Knoll A (Natural)	–	–	–	0	4	(?)	–
Knoll B (Natural)	–	–	–	0	1	(?)	–
Knoll C	40	5	3	8	8	Middle Woodland.	Completely excavated.

Notes: Located on ridge crest at western margin of Illinois River, in Calhoun County, where Kampsville Creek junctures with the main valley. Unsystematic excavations were conducted by L. Gibson in Mounds 4 and 5; the remainder of the group was completely excavated by G. Perino and J. Buikstra in 1969.

Sources: Buikstra 1972; Perino 1968, 1973b; Titterington n.d.[a].

Gracey Mound Group

Mound no.	Dimensions (ft)			Minimum number of individuals		Cultural affiliation	Excavation techniques
	L	W	H	Middle Woodland	Total		
1-4	–	–	–	–	–	–	Not excavated.
5	–	–	–	1	1	Middle Woodland.	Trenched.

Notes: Located on bluff crest overlooking Macoupin Valley, in Greene County, 30 miles from juncture of Illinois and Macoupin valleys. Mound 5 was excavated by Harold Spencer and students, Blackburn College, in 1952. Group consists of 4 mounds and possibly one more that was destroyed by a road cut.

Sources: Farnsworth personal communication and 1973.

Hagen Mound Group

Mound no.	Dimensions (ft)			Minimum number of individuals		Cultural affiliation	Excavation techniques
	L	W	H	Middle Woodland	Total		
1	Oval		3-5	1	2	Middle Woodland + possibly some burials of later age.	Incompletely excavated.
"Government Marker" Mound	–	–	–	0	5	Late Archaic or Early Woodland, and Late Woodland.	Incompletely excavated.

Notes: Located on bluff crest at western margin of Illinois Valley, in Calhoun County. Titterington reports that the group consisted of more than 6 mounds; 6 of these, including Mound 1, were oval and 3-5 ft high. Mound excavations were conducted by Walter Wadlow, L. Gibson, and P. F. Titterington, ca. 1945.

Sources: Titterington 1947, n.d.[a]; Struever 1968b:290; Perino 1961:53.

Hardin Mound Group

Mound no.	Dimensions (ft)			Minimum number of individuals		Cultural affiliation	Excavation techniques
	L	W	H	Middle Woodland	Total		
1	100	93	19	4	9	Middle Woodland + later (?) intrusive burials.	10- to 25-ft-wide trench.

Hardin Mound Group (Cont.).

Mound no.	Dimensions (ft)			Minimum number of individuals		Cultural affiliation	Excavation techniques
	L	W	H	Middle Woodland	Total		
2	47	26	3	–	–	–	Not excavated.
3	93	84	16	–	–	–	Not excavated.
4	25	21	1½	–	–	–	Not excavated.
5	21	15	2	–	–	–	Not excavated.

Notes: Located on bluff crest at western margin of Illinois Valley, in Calhoun County. Excavated by James D. Middleton in 1888.

Sources: Correspondence of James D. Middleton with Cyrus Thomas, in files of Smithsonian Institution, National Anthropological Archives, dated 8/22/1888 and 8/26/1888; Middleton 1888; Thomas 1889, 1894:129-131; Struever 1968b:291.

Hazelherst (Hazelherst-Brundies) Mound Group

Mound no.	Dimensions (ft)			Minimum number of individuals		Cultural affiliation	Excavation techniques
	L	W	H	Middle Woodland	Total		
1	30	30	4	2	2	Middle Woodland.	Excavated by W. L. Wadlow.
2-6	–	–	–	–	–	–	Not excavated.
7	20	20	3	0	2	Late Woodland.	Excavated by W. L. Wadlow.
8	30	30	4	5	5	Middle Woodland.	Excavated by L. M. Gibson.

Notes: Located on bluff crest at western margin of Illinois Valley, in Calhoun County. Excavated in 1951.
Sources: Fecht 1955; Struever 1968b:294-295; Perino n.d. [b].

Helm Mound Group

Mound no.	Dimensions (ft)			Minimum number of individuals		Cultural affiliation	Excavation techniques
	L	W	H	Middle Woodland	Total		
1	90	30	4	2	17	Middle Woodland primary mound; Late Woodland secondary mound.	–
2	40	40	4	2	2	Middle Woodland (?).	Earlier excavators removed and reinterred a number of burials.
3	96	30	3½	0	9	Late Woodland (?); burials were flexed.	–
4	34	34	4	1	1	Middle Woodland.	Excavated by amateur archeologist Raymond Long in 1930's.
5-6	Elliptical			–	–	Outline suggests Late Woodland affiliation.	Not excavated.

Notes: Located on bluff crest at western margin of Illinois Valley, in Pike County. Excavated incompletely by Gregory H. Perino ca. 1955.
Sources: Perino n.d.[a]; Struever 1960:196-197, 1968b:296-297.

Kamp Mound Group

Mound no.	Dimensions (ft)			Minimum number of individuals		Cultural affiliation	Excavation techniques
	L	W	H	Middle Woodland	Total		
1	~100	~100	20	–	–	–	Not excavated.
2	60	60	3½	4	4	Middle Woodland (?).	Tested by J. L. B. Taylor, 1928.
3	75	75	5	1	1	Middle Woodland.	Tested by J. L. B. Taylor, 1928.
4	75	75	4½	3	3	Middle Woodland.	Tested by J. L. B. Taylor, 1928.
5	90	90	12	–	–	–	Not excavated.
6-7[a]	250	100	17	–	–	–	Not excavated.
8	325	150	20	–	–	–	Not excavated.
9[a]	260	135	16	5[b]	5[b]	Middle Woodland.[c]	2/3 excavated by S. Struever, 1958-1959.
10	125	125	20	–	–	–	Not excavated.

Notes: Situated on floodplain of Illinois River at mouth of Woods Creek, in Calhoun County, within 100 yd of western bluffs of Illinois Valley and ca. 500 yd from river.

Sources: Griffin and Morgan 1941:35-39; Struever 1960; Crane and Griffin 1962; Buikstra 1972.

[a] Biconical.

[b] Based on Buikstra's reevaluation.

[c] C^{14} dates from crypt in primary mound: A.D. 190±100 (M-1038; charcoal inside pot), A.D. 10±75 (M-1039; charcoal inside pot), A.D. 140±75 (M-1041; log from tomb wall). C^{14} date from charcoal in pit beneath primary mound: 30 B.C.±75 (M-1040).

Ben Klunk Mound Group

Mound no.	Dimensions (ft)			Minimum number of individuals		Cultural affiliation*	Excavation techniques
	L	W	H	Middle Woodland	Total		
1	35	32	6	0	1	(?)	Not excavated by Middleton; earlier excavators had discovered a burial.
2	48	40	4½	–	–	–	Not excavated.
3	55	47	3½	–	–	–	Not excavated.
4	30	20	3	0	3	(?)	Undisturbed prior to Middleton's investigation.
5	58	56	4	–	–	–	Not excavated.
6	–	–	–	–	–	–	Not excavated.

Notes: Located on ridge crest at western margin of Illinois River, in Calhoun County, where Kampsville Creek junctures with the main valley. The mound sequence of Perino's sketch map (1973a:59) was renumbered in Fig. 2 to accommodate a newly recognized mound which is third in the sequence from east to west. Mounds 1-5 of Fig. 2 are probably the same as Middleton's Mounds 1-5. Observations for Mounds 1-5 in the table above are Middleton's.

Sources: Middleton 1888; Thomas 1894:128-129; Perino 1973a:58-59.

Pete Klunk Mound Group

Mound no.	Dimensions (ft)			Minimum number of individuals		Cultural affiliation	Excavation techniques
	L	W	H	Middle Woodland	Total		
1	76	56	10	91	92	Middle Woodland + intrusive Late Woodland burial: C[14] date of A.D. 175±75 (M-1161) from burned tree stump beneath mound.	Completely excavated.
2	70	50	8	50	50	Middle Woodland.	Completely excavated.
3[a]	–	–	–	0	1	(?)	–
4[a]	–	–	–	0	3	—	–
5	38	28	3½	40	43	Middle Woodland + 3 flexed intrusive Late Woodland burials.	Completely excavated.
Natural knoll (50 ft. N of Md. 5)	–	–	–	0	5	(?)	–
6	55	44	6	31	43	Middle Woodland + intrusive Late Woodland burials.	Completely excavated.
Crematory A (20 ft. S of Md. 6)	–	–	–	0	1	Late Woodland.	–
Crematory B (50 ft. S of Md. 6)	–	–	–	0	3	Late Woodland.	–
7	45	55	5½	38 +1 fetus	108 +1 fetus	Middle Woodland mound overlying Archaic mound with 62 burials, + 8 Late Woodland burials.	Completely excavated.
8	60	27	3½	0	47	Late Woodland; C[14] date of A.D. 600±110 (M-1355) from wood charcoal in crematory situated between primary mounds.	Completely excavated.
9 (Middleton's Md. 7)	16	16	5/6	0	3	Late Woodland.	Completely excavated by Perino; Middleton's excavation accounts for 1 individual.
15 ft. N of Md. 9	–	–	–	0	2	Late Woodland.	–
10 (Middleton's Md. 6)	20	20	1⅓	0	9	Late Woodland; C[14] date of A.D. 780±120 (M-1356) from charcoal in a crematory.	Completely excavated by Perino; Middleton's excavation accounts for 2 individuals.
11 (Middleton's Md. 5)	45	45	3½	122 +1 fetus	122 +1 fetus	Middle Woodland.	Completely excavated by Perino; Middleton's excavation accounts for at least 3 individuals.

Pete Klunk Mound Group (Cont.).

Mound no.	Dimensions (ft)			Minimum number of individuals		Cultural affiliation	Excavation techniques
	L	W	H	Middle Woodland	Total		
12	40	40	3	1	1	Middle Woodland sub-floor tomb and primary mound (identification based on morphology only) + Late Woodland secondary mound cap.	Completely excavated.
13	40	40	2	2	2	Middle Woodland sub-floor tomb and primary mound + Late Woodland secondary cap.	Completely excavated.
Middleton's Md. 2[b]	25	20	1½	0	0	(?)	Excavated by Middleton.
14 (Middleton's Md. 1)	65	45	5	0	29	15 Late Woodland-Mississippi individuals + 4 Archaic individuals in charnal pit beneath mound + 10 individuals recovered by Middleton.	All but 1/10 of mound destroyed prior to Perino's excavation.

Notes: Located on bluff crest at western margin of Illinois River, in Calhoun County, where Kampsville Creek junctures the main valley. Some mounds were partially excavated by Middleton in 1888. Mound group was completely excavated by Perino in 1960. Evaluation of skeletal series by Buikstra (1972 and personal communication) augmented some of the burial counts appearing in Perino's field reports.

Sources: Perino 1968, 1973a; Buikstra 1972; Middleton 1888; Thomas 1894:126-128; Crane and Griffin 1963, 1964, 1966.

[a] Natural knoll.

[b] Not observed by Perino; probably a natural knoll.

Knight Mound Group

Mound no.	Dimensions (ft)[a]			Minimum number of individuals		Cultural affiliation	Excavation techniques
	L	W	H	Middle Woodland	Total		
1	50	25	⩾6	0	19	Early Late Woodland.	Completely excavated.
2	⩾60	⩾60	~5	0	52	Early Late Woodland.	Extensively excavated by W. L. Wadlow; trenched by P. F. Titterington.
3	~35	~20	~5	6	17	Middle Woodland in part, possibly only the red clay primary (?) mound; yellow loess cap probably entirely an early Late Woodland contribution.	Attacked several times by W. L. Wadlow.
4	48	38	⩾6	23	24	Central pit clearly Middle Woodland and probably individuals at or near base of mound as well; mound superstructure in part Middle Woodland, possibly also early Late Woodland.	Pit 6 ft in diameter excavated ca. 1900; extensively excavated by Wadlow's father and L. M. Gibson; 25- and 10-ft-wide trenches excavated by P. F. Titterington.
5	55-60	42	10$\frac{1}{3}$	22	28	Central pit is Middle Woodland; some burials in upper mound fill are early Late Woodland, others possibly Middle Woodland.	Trenched by P. F. Titterington.
6	Second smallest of Mounds 1-13			12	12	Subfloor pit is Middle Woodland; upper part of mound possibly of early Late Woodland age.	Excavated by L. M. Gibson.
7	–	–	–	5	5	Middle Woodland (?); no associated artifacts; assignment based on presence of central rectangular subfloor burial pit.	Excavated with slip scraper and team by W. L. Wadlow.
8	50	40	6	13	13	Middle Woodland; C[14] date of A.D. 250±150 (M-164) obtained for *Busycon* shell.	20-ft trench excavated by W. L. Wadlow and father; excavation continued by P. F. Titterington; none of the poorly preserved skeletal remains were saved.
Unmounded burial near Md. 8	–	–	–	0	1	(?); burial was flexed, probably Late Woodland.	–
9	–	–	–	–	–	–	No information.

Knight Mound Group (Cont.).

Mound no.	Dimensions (ft)			Minimum number of individuals		Cultural affiliation	Excavation techniques
	L	W	H	Middle Woodland	Total		
10	–	–	–	–	–	(?) Possibly Middle Woodland based on inclusions in fill.	Test pitted by W. L. Wadlow; no information available concerning burials or provenience of artifacts.
11-13	–	–	–	–	–	–	No information.
14	50	38	9½	0	1	Archaic (?); Griffin *et al.* (1970:89) suggest that 4 Archaic knives may have been used by later people; but no sherds recovered.	20-ft-wide trench from one side to 5 ft beyond center.
15 (Natural knoll ?)	33	22	–	0	0	–	10-ft-wide trench 2/3 of way through knoll.
16	60	60	20-25	17	28	Middle Woodland + possibly later peripheral burials.	About 2/3 excavated by P. F. Titterington; cross-trenched.
17	Oval, ~35?	–	3-5	0	11	Late Woodland (Jersey Bluff).	Incompletely excavated by P. F. Titterington.
18, 20	Oval	–	Low	–	–	Outlines suggest Late Woodland origin.	Not excavated.
19	Oval	–	Low	0	1	Early Late Woodland.	Dug by W. L. Wadlow.
21	Oval ~35?	–	3-5	0	6	Late Woodland.	North end opened by P. F. Titterington.
22	52	38	9	12	22	Middle Woodland + flexed Late Woodland (Jersey Bluff) burials near top of mound.	Excavated by P. F. Titterington.
23-25	Oval	–	Low	–	–	Outlines suggest Late Woodland origin.	Not excavated.
26	"Large conical"			–	–	Thought to be Middle Woodland.	Not excavated.

Notes: Located on three ridges at mouth of Fox Creek Hollow, east side of Mississippi Valley, in Calhoun County, about 8 miles west of Kampsville and just outside defined research universe. According to definitions of this paper there are actually three mound groups, consisting of (1) Mounds 1-13, (2) Mounds 14-15, and (3) Mounds 16-26. Only the first and third groups have Middle Woodland burials. Most of the mounds were excavated incompletely during the 1940's primarily by W. L. Wadlow and father, L. M. Gibson, and P. F. Titterington. Only Titterington's excavations were controlled, with systematic recording of data; information about other excavations are based on random observations by Titterington.

Sources: Titterington n.d.[b]; Griffin, Flanders, and Titterington 1970; McKern, Titterington, and Griffin 1945; Crane 1956; Wilkinson 1971.

[a]General description for Mounds 1-15, 22, and 26: circular to widely oval, 30-50 ft in length and width, 6-12 ft high. General description for Mounds 17-21, 23-25: long, low, oval, 3-5 ft high.

L'Orient Mound Group

Mound no.	Dimensions (ft)			Minimum number of individuals		Cultural affiliation	Excavation techniques
	L	W	H	Middle Woodland	Total		
1	–	–	–	24	24	Middle Woodland (?).	About 2/3 excavated.
2	–	–	–	29	29	Middle Woodland (?).	Completely excavated.

Notes: Situated on bluff crest at western margin of Illinois Valley, in Calhoun County. Excavated by Gregory H. Perino in 1972.
Source: J. Buikstra personal communication.

Meppen (Baalman-Pehm) Mound Group

Mound no.	Dimensions (ft)			Minimum number of individuals		Cultural affiliation	Excavation techniques
	L	W	H	Middle Woodland	Total		
1	40	40	7	2	17	Middle Woodland and Middle Mississippi.	Excavated by W. Fecht, G. Perino, W. Wadlow, L. Foersterling, D. Alt, and V. Lischer.
Burials between Mounds 1 and 2	–	–	–	0	1	(?)	Excavated by R. North.
2	25	25	4	–	–	(?)	Had been pitted prior to investigations in 1951.
3	17	17	3	0	6	(?)	Excavated by G. Perino.
4	25	25	5	2	3	Middle Woodland + possible intrusive burials.	Trenched by R. North; pitted by G. Perino.
5	Circular		–	0	1	(?)	Excavated by G. Perino.
6	20	20	3	1	5	Middle Woodland (?); 4 burials reported as intrusive.	Excavated by G. Perino. *et al.*
7	15	15	2	0	2	(?)	Excavated by C. Dunford.
8	35	15	1½	1	10	Middle Woodland (?) + 9 intrusive burials.	Excavated by G. Perino.
9	35	15	1½	0	2	(?)	Excavated by C. Gerfen.
10	35	15	1½	1	1	Middle Woodland.	Trenched by G. Perino.
11	Circular		1	3	3	Middle Woodland (?).	Excavated by A. Baalman's son.
12	Circular		1	–	–	–	Unexcavated.

Notes: Located on bluff crest at western margin of Illinois Valley, in Calhoun County. Only the mounds on Pehm and Baalman properties are included in definition of this mound group; mounds on Hazelherst and Brundies property allocated to Hazelherst group. Excavations carried out primarily by members of Greater St. Louis Archaeological Society in 1951 were in general unsystematic and incomplete, with inadequate records. Probably most burials recovered were of Middle Woodland origin. Five burials were excavated from a mound on the Pehm property by C. McDonald in 1944.
Sources: Fecht 1955; Struever 1968b:341-344; Perino 1968:40, n.d.[b]; McDonald 1944.

Meredosia-Hilderbrand Mound Group

| Mound no. | Dimensions (ft) | | | Minimum number of individuals | | Cultural affiliation | Excavation techniques |
	L	W	H	Middle Woodland	Total		
Hilder-brand	140	70	5	0	0	(?)Mound fill contained Middle Woodland habitation debris, but no structural features or burials encountered in excavation.	Trenched.
Meredo-sia 1		"Huge"		0	0	Middle Woodland.	Salvage excavations carried out by R. Jenkins, an amateur, over period of 4-5 years as mound was in process of being leveled.
Meredo-sia 2-13	–	–	–	–	–	–	Unexcavated.

Notes: Located along eastern shore of Meredosia Lake in Illinois Valley bottomland east of the present river channel, in Morgan County. Hilderbrand mound excavated by J. L. B. Taylor in 1928.
Sources: Griffin and Morgan 1941:28-29; Struever 1968b:345-348; Struever and Perino 1968.

Merrigan Mound Group

| Mound no. | Dimensions (ft) | | | Minimum number of individuals | | Cultural affiliation | Excavation techniques |
	L	W	H	Middle Woodland	Total		
1	175	150	~16	3	6	Middle Woodland + later (?) flexed intrusive burials.	Center shaft and bulldozer; most of mound periphery unexamined.
2-4	–	–	–	–	–	–	Not excavated.

Notes: Located on Illinois River bottoms 300 yd west of present river channel, in Calhoun County. William McAdams excavated central feature of Mound 1 in 1881; Wadlow and LaDassor reexcavated central feature and bulldozed off top of the mound in 1950. K. Farnsworth (personal communication) reports existence of three mounds in addition to Mound 1.
Sources: Struever 1970; McAdams 1884:684; Wadlow and LaDassor 1951.

Montezuma (McEvers) Mound Group

| Mound no. | Dimensions (ft) | | | Minimum number of individuals | | Cultural affiliation | Excavation techniques |
	L	W	H	Middle Woodland	Total		
1	130	130	24-28	7	7	Middle Woodland.	Tunneling and trenching; trench excavated in part by team and scraper and plow; central tomb excavated (in 1905); Perino also excavated a trench.
2	100	100	9	3	3	(?)	Trench from one side of mound to center in 1905; Perino cross-trenched the mound.

Montezuma (McEvers) Mound Group (Cont.).

Mound no.	Dimensions (ft)			Minimum number of individuals		Cultural affiliation	Excavation techniques
	L	W	H	Middle Woodland	Total		
3	105	105	6	0	0	(?)	Trench; at least 20 ft wide at center of mound.
4	100	100	8½	3	3	(?)	Trench; 24 ft wide at center of mound
5	125	125	12	13	13	Middle Woodland.	7-ft-wide trench.
6	20	20	3	3	4	(?)	Central area 13 ft wide excavated in 1905; Perino completed excavation.
7	25	25	5	22	22	Middle Woodland.	South side excavated to 3 ft north of center in 1905; Perino completed excavation.
8	–	–	–	11	11	(?)	About ½ of mound excavated.
9	–	–	8	1	1	(?)	Trenched.
10	72	72	6⅓	1	3	Middle Woodland + later (?) intrusive flexed burials in mound superstructure.	Trenched.
11	68 (Oval)	?	7	2	5	Middle Woodland + later (?) flexed burials in mound superstructure.	–
12	48	48	4	1	3	Middle Woodland + later (?) intrusive flexed burials near mound surface.	–
13[a]	–	–	–	2	2	Middle Woodland (?).	–
14	45	45	3	1	1	Middle Woodland.	–
15	60	60	6½	1	1	Middle Woodland.	–

Notes: Located on bluff crest at western margin of Illinois Valley, in Pike County. Mounds 1-8 incompletely excavated by McEvers, Bushnell, and Wolfing and/or Fowke in 1905; G. Perino excavated Mounds 9-15 in 1955-56 not searching for peripherally located burials.

Sources: Perino n.d.[a]; Fowke 1905; Bayliss 1907; Bushnell 1905; Struever 1960:193-194, 1968b:354-356.

[a]A natural knoll.

Mound House Mound Group:

Notes: Situated in floodplain of Illinois River about ¼ mile east of present channel, in Greene County. Consists of three (?) unexcavated mounds. Because of location in major Middle Woodland habitation site, mounds are assumed to be of Middle Woodland cultural affiliation.

Source: Struever 1968b:359-360.

Naples Abbott Mound Group

Mound no.	Dimensions (ft)			Minimum number of individuals		Cultural affiliation	Excavation techniques
	L	W	H	Middle Woodland	Total		
1[a]	250	180	17	2	2	Middle Woodland (?); mound fill contained Middle Woodland sherds.	River cut inspected by Taylor; little or no excavation.
15[b]	60	60	6	2	2	Middle Woodland (?); mound fill contained Middle Woodland sherds.	Center shaft 8 ft square dug by Henderson.

Notes: Located on natural levee on east side of Illinois River, in Scott County. The group consists of 9 mounds. John G. Henderson explored Mound 15 ca. 1880. J. L. B. Taylor inspected river cut in Mound 1 (his number) in 1928.

Sources: Henderson 1884; Griffin and Morgan 1941:29-33; Struever 1968b:362-365.

[a]Taylor's no. This was Henderson's Mound 13.

[b]Henderson's no.

Naples Castle Mound Group

Mound no.	Dimensions (ft)			Minimum number of individuals		Cultural affiliation	Excavation techniques
	L	W	H	Middle Woodland	Total		
6[a]	136	136	15	2	2	Middle Woodland (?); mound fill contained Middle Woodland sherds.	Tunnelling, trenching, and center shaft by Henderson.
7[a]	Oblong shape, due to river action.			0	0	(?)	Shaft excavated into mound by Henderson; also tested by Taylor.

Notes: Situated on east bank of Illinois River at mouth of Mauvaise Terre Creek in Scott County. The group consists of two mounds. John G. Henderson excavated in both mounds ca. 1880, and J. L. B. Taylor tested Mound 7 in 1928.

Sources: Henderson 1884; Struever 1968b:366; Griffin and Morgan 1941:33.

[a]As numbered by Henderson.

Naples Chambers Mound Group

Mound no.	Dimensions (ft)			Minimum number of individuals		Cultural affiliation	Excavation techniques
	L	W	H	Middle Woodland	Total		
1	132	98	10	1	1	Middle Woodland.	Trenches and tunnels.
2	86	86	11	1	1	Middle Woodland.	Center digging.
3	90	90	11$\frac{1}{3}$	9	9	Middle Woodland.	8-ft-square center shaft.
4	65	65	4$\frac{2}{3}$	1	1	(?)	8-ft-square center shaft.
5	50	50	3½	0	0	(?)	(?)

Notes: Situated on sand ridge in Illinois Valley floodplain about ¾ mile east of present river channel, in Scott County. Excavated ca. 1880 by John G. Henderson.

Sources: Henderson 1884; Struever 1968b:367-368.

Parsell Mound Group

Mound no.	Dimensions (ft)			Minimum number of individuals		Cultural affiliation	Excavation techniques
	L	W	H	Middle Woodland	Total		
Jy° 190	77	31	8	0	62	Late Woodland (Jersey Bluff)	–
Jy° 191	65	38	5-6	0	39	Late Woodland (Jersey Bluff).	–
Jy° 192	52	35	–	0	19	Late Woodland (Jersey Bluff).	–
Jy° 195	52	22	ca.4	0	24	Late Woodland (Jersey Bluff).	–
Jy° 196[a]	–	–	–	0	0	–	Tested.
Jy° 199	>29	>16½	≥5	5	70	Some Hopewell pottery associated with burials; of probable Middle Woodland burials, 4 are extended; mound contents primarily Jersey Bluff.	–

Notes: Located on bluff crest at eastern margin of Illinois Valley, in Jersey County. Excavated during 1940's by P. F. Titterington. Hopewell pot found at head of burial in Jy° 199 by amateur Stuart Parsell in 1934. Mounds Jy° 189, 193, 194, 197, 198 were not excavated.

Sources: Shalkop 1949; Titterington 1935:7, n.d.[c]; Griffin 1941:218-219; Griffin and Morgan 1941:5.

[a]May be a natural knoll.

Peisker Mound Group

Mound no.	Dimensions (ft)			Minimum number of individuals		Cultural affiliation[a]	Excavation techniques
	L	W	H	Middle Woodland	Total		
1	100	100	10	3	3	Middle Woodland.	About ¾ of mound excavated; central tomb previously disturbed.
2	135	100	10	44	44	Middle Woodland.	About 2/3 excavated.
3	72	72	4	11	11	Middle Woodland.	Only the tomb was excavated.

Notes: Located in Illinois Valley floodplain, on beach adjacent to west side of present river channel, in Calhoun County. Excavated by Gregory H. Perino in 1962-63. Burial counts based on evaluation of skeletal series by J. Buikstra. Excludes submound Early Woodland burials.

Sources: Perino 1964, 1966a, 1966b, 1966c; Buikstra 1972; Struever 1968b:142-143, 157-158, 373-376; Crane and Griffin 1966, 1968, 1972b; Wittry 1964.

[a]See Table 1 for submound C^{14} dates.

Pilot's Peak Mound Group

Mound no.	Dimensions (ft)			Minimum number of individuals		Cultural affiliation	Excavation techniques
	L	W	H	Middle Woodland	Total		
1	90	50	9	7	16	Middle Woodland + later (?) flexed intrusive burials.	10-ft-wide trench.
2	75	75	12	–	–	–	Previously disturbed; not excavated by Perino.
3	60	60	10	2	2	Middle Woodland.	10-ft-square center shaft.
4	50	50	7	0	0	(?)	Tested with center shaft; excavation terminated due to prior disturbance.
5	33	33	2	–	–	–	Previously excavated.

Notes: Located on bluff crest at western margin of Illinois Valley, in Pike County. Excavated by G. Perino in 1955-56.
Sources: Perino n.d.; Struever 1960:195, 1968b:377.

Robertson Mound Group

Mound no.	Dimensions (ft)			Minimum number of individuals		Cultural affiliation	Excavation techniques
	L	W	H	Middle Woodland	Total		
1	300	150	4	0	3	(?) Mound fill contained Middle Woodland pottery.	Not reported; incomplete.
2	300	150	4	0	1	(?)	Not reported; very limited testing.

Notes: Located in Illinois Valley floodplain east of present river channel, in Scott County. Mound group named by Struever. Griffin and Morgan called this the Naples Castle mound group, Mounds 1 and 2. Excavations by J. L. B. Taylor in 1928.
Sources: Griffin and Morgan 1941:33-34; Struever 1968b:384.

Swartz (Little Blue Creek) Mound Group

Mound no.	Dimensions (ft)			Minimum number of individuals		Cultural affiliation	Excavation techniques
	L	W	H	Middle Woodland	Total		
1	80	80	9	3	3	Middle Woodland.	Center pit excavated into central tomb.
2-3	–	–	–	–	–	–	Unexcavated

Notes: Situated on bluff crest at western margin of Illinois Valley, in Pike County. Mound 1 excavated by G. Perino, 1955-56. Struever reports that the group consists of 3(?) mounds.
Sources: Perino n.d.[a]; Struever 1968b:393.

References Cited

Asch, Nancy B., Richard I. Ford, and David L. Asch
1972   *Paleoethnobotany of the Koster Site: The Archaic Horizons.* Illinois State Museum Reports of Investigations, No. 24, and Illinois Valley Archaeological Program Research Papers, Vol. 6. Springfield.

Ascher, Robert
1959   A prehistoric population estimate using midden analysis and two population models. *Southwest. J. Anthropol.* 15(2):168-178.

Barclay, George W.
1958   *Techniques of Population Analysis.* New York, John Wiley & Sons, Inc.

Bartholomew, George A., Jr., and Joseph B. Birdsell
1953   Ecology and the protohominids. *Am. Anthropol.* 55(4):481-498.

Baumhoff, Martin A.
1963   *Ecological Determinants of Aboriginal California Populations.* University of California Publications in American Archaeology and Ethnology, 49(2):155-236. Berkeley, University of California Press.

Bayliss, Clara Kern
1907   The McEvers Mounds, Pike Co., Illinois. *Rec. of the Past* 6(1):21-27.

Binford, Lewis R.
1968   Post-Pleistocene adaptations. In *New Perspectives in Archeology,* Sally R. Binford and Lewis R. Binford (Eds.), pp. 313-341. Chicago, Aldine Publishing Company.
1971   Mortuary practices: their study and their potential. In *Approaches to the Social Dimensions of Mortuary Practices,* James A. Brown (Ed.), pp. 6-29. Memoirs of the Society for American Archaeology, No. 25. Washington.

Birdsell, Joseph B.
1953   Some environmental and cultural factors influencing the structure of Australian aboriginal populations. *Am. Naturalist* 87(834):171-207.
1957   Some population problems involving Pleistocene man. *In* Population Studies: Animal Ecology and Demography. *Cold Spring Harbor Symp. Quant. Biol.* 22:47-68.
1958   On population structure in generalized hunting and collecting populations. *Evolution* 12(2):189-205.
1968   Some predictions for the Pleistocene based on equilibrium systems among recent hunter-gatherers. In *Man the Hunter,* Richard B. Lee and Irven DeVore (Eds.), pp. 229-240. Chicago, Aldine Publishing Company.

Blakely, Robert L.
1971   Comparison of the mortality profiles of Archaic, Middle Woodland, and Middle Mississippian skeletal populations. *Am. J. Phys. Anthropol.* 34(1):43-54.

Boserup, Ester
1965   *The Conditions of Agricultural Growth: The Economics of Agrarian Change Under Population Pressure.* Chicago, Aldine Publishing Company.

Brothwell, Don
1972   Paleodemography and earlier British populations. *World Archaeol.* 4(1):75-87.

Brown, James A.
1965   *The Prairie Peninsula: An Interaction Area in the Eastern United States.* Ph.D. dissertation, Department of Anthropology, University of Chicago. Chicago.

Buikstra, Jane E.
1972   *Hopewell in the Lower Illinois River Valley: A Regional Approach to the Study of Biological Variability and Mortuary Activities.* Ph.D. dissertation, Department of Anthropology, University of Chicago. Chicago. To be published as Northwestern University Archeological Program Scientific Papers, No. 2.

Buikstra, Jane E., and Lynne Goldstein
1973   *The Perrins Ledge Crematory.* Illinois State Museum Reports of Investigations, No. 28, and Illinois Valley Archaeological Program Research Papers, Vol. 8. Springfield.

Bushnell, David I.
1905   Partial excavation of the N. D. McEvers mound. *Rec. of the Past* 4(7):202-205.

Cain, Stanley A.
1944   *Foundations of Plant Geography.* New York, Harper and Brothers.

Carneiro, Robert L.
1967   On the relationship between size of population and complexity of social organization. *Southwest. J. Anthropol.* 23(3):234-243.

Carrier, N. H.
1958   A note on the estimation of mortality and other population characteristics given deaths by age. *Pop. Studies* 12(2):149-163.

Caughley, Graeme
1966   Mortality patterns in mammals. *Ecology* 47(6):906-918.

Cole, Fay-Cooper, and Thorne Deuel
1937   *Rediscovering Illinois: Archaeological Explorations In and Around Fulton County.* Chicago, The University of Chicago Press.

Cook, Della C.
1971   *Patterns of Nutritional Stress in Some Illinois Woodland Populations.* M.A. research paper, Department of Anthropology, University of Chicago. Chicago.

Cook, Sherburne F., and Robert F. Heizer
1965   *The Quantitative Approach to the Relation Between Population and Settlement Size.* Reports of the University of California Archaeological Survey, No. 64. Berkeley, University of California Archaeological Research Facility.
1968   Relationships among houses, settlement areas, and population in aboriginal California. In *Settlement Archaeology,* K. C. Chang (Ed.), pp. 79-116. Palo Alto, National Press Books.

Cook, Sherburne F., and A. E. Treganza
1950   *The Quantitative Investigation of Indian Mounds, With Special Reference to the Relation of the Physical Components to the Prob-*

able Material Culture. University of California Publications in American Archaeology and Ethnology, 40(5):223-262. Berkeley, University of California Press.

Corwin, Richard Noel
1968   *Faunas From Four Archaeological Sites in the Lower Illinois Valley.* M.S. thesis, Department of Biological Sciences, Illinois State University. Normal, Ill.

Crane, H. R.
1956   University of Michigan radiocarbon dates I. *Science* 124(3224):664-672.

Crane, H. R., and James B. Griffin
1958a   University of Michigan radiocarbon dates II. *Science* 127(3306):1098-1105.

1958b   University of Michigan radiocarbon dates III. *Science* 128(3332):1117-1123.

1959   University of Michigan radiocarbon dates IV. *Am. J. Sci. Radiocarbon Supp.* 1:173-198.

1962   University of Michigan radiocarbon dates VII. *Radiocarbon* 4:183-203.

1963   University of Michigan radiocarbon dates VIII. *Radiocarbon* 5:228-253.

1964   University of Michigan radiocarbon dates IX. *Radiocarbon* 6:1-24.

1965   University of Michigan radiocarbon dates X. *Radiocarbon* 7:123-152.

1966   University of Michigan radiocarbon dates XI. *Radiocarbon* 8:256-285.

1968   University of Michigan radiocarbon dates XII. *Radiocarbon* 10(1):61-114.

1970   University of Michigan radiocarbon dates XIII. *Radiocarbon* 12(1):161-180.

1972a   University of Michigan radiocarbon dates XIV. *Radiocarbon* 14(1):155-194

1972b   University of Michigan radiocarbon dates XV. *Radiocarbon* 14(1):195-222.

Deuel, Thorne
1952   The Hopewellian community. In *Hopewellian Communities in Illinois,* Thorne Deuel (Ed.), pp. 249-265. Illinois State Museum Scientific Papers, Vol. 5, No. 6. Springfield.

Dobyns, Henry F.
1966   Estimating aboriginal American population, 1. An appraisal of techniques with a new hemispheric estimate. *Current Anthropol.* 7(4):395-416.

Durkheim, Emile
1933   *The Division of Labor in Society,* George Simpson (Trans.). Glencoe, Ill., The Free Press of Glencoe.

Farnsworth, Kenneth B.
1973   *An Archaeological Survey of the Macoupin Valley.* Illinois State Museum Reports of Investigations, No. 26, and Illinois Valley Archaeological Program Research Papers, Vol. 7. Springfield.

Fecht, William G.
1955   Mound explorations at Meppen, Illinois. *Central States Archaeol. J.* 2(1):29-34.

1961   The Snyders mound group and village site. *Central States Archaeol. J.* 8(3):84-93.

1969   Additional information from the Snyders site, Calhoun County, Illinois. *Central States Archaeol. J.* 16(2):63-77.

Fehrenbacher, J. B., and C. E. Downey
1966   *Soil Survey: Jersey County, Illinois.* University of Illinois Agricultural Experiment Station Soil Report, No. 84. Urbana, Ill.

Flanders, Richard E., and James B. Griffin
1970   The Norton Mound Group, Kent County, Michigan. In *The Burial Complexes of the Knight and Norton Mounds in Illinois and Michigan,* by James B. Griffin, Richard E. Flanders, and Paul F. Titterington, pp. 125-189. Memoirs of the Museum of Anthropology, No. 2. Ann Arbor, University of Michigan.

Flannery, Kent V.
1968   Archeological systems theory and early Mesoamerica. In *Anthropological Archeology in the Americas,* Betty J. Meggers (Ed.), pp. 67-87. Washington, Anthropological Society of Washington.

Fowke, Gerard
1905   The Montezuma Mounds. *Missouri Hist. Soc. Coll.* 2(5):1-16. St. Louis.

Geertz, Clifford
1963   *Agricultural Involution: The Processes of Ecological Change in Indonesia.* Association of Asian Studies Monographs and Papers, No. 11. Berkeley, University of California Press.

Glassow, Michael A.
1967   Considerations in estimating prehistoric California coastal populations. *Am. Antiq.* 32(3):354-359.

Goldstein, Lynne
n.d.   *An Analysis of Plummets in the Lower Illinois Valley.* Manuscript on file at the Department of Anthropology, Northwestern University. Evanston.

Griffin, James B.
1941   Additional Hopewell material from Illinois. *Indiana Hist. Soc. Prehist. Res. Ser.* 2(3):163-224.

1952   A preview of the ceramic relationships of the Snyders site, Calhoun County, Illinois. In *The Snyders Site, Calhoun County, Illinois,* pp. 14-18. St. Louis, The Greater St. Louis Archaeological Society.

1965   Hopewell and the dark black glass. *Michigan Archaeol.* 11(3-4):115-155.

1970   Introduction. In *The Burial Complexes of the Knight and Norton Mounds in Illinois and Michigan,* by James B. Griffin, Richard E. Flanders, and Paul F. Titterington, pp. 1-10. Memoirs of the Museum of Anthropology, No. 2. Ann Arbor, University of Michigan.

Griffin, James B., and Richard G. Morgan (Eds.)
1941   *Contributions to the Archaeology of the Illinois River Valley.* Transactions of the American Philosophical Society, Vol. 32, Part 1. Philadelphia.

Griffin, James B., Richard E. Flanders, and Paul F. Titterington
1970   The Knight mound group, Calhoun County, Illinois. In *The Burial Complexes of the Knight and Norton Mounds in Illinois and Michigan,* by James B. Griffin, Richard E. Flanders, and Paul F. Titterington, pp.

11-123. Memoirs of the Museum of Anthropology, No. 2. Ann Arbor, University of Michigan.

Hainline, Jane
1965 Culture and biological adaptation. *Am. Anthropol.* 67(5):1174-1197.

Harner, Michael J.
1970 Population pressure and the social evolution of agriculturalists. *Southwest. J. Anthropol.* 26(1):67-86.

Haviland, William A.
1965 Prehistoric settlement at Tikal, Guatemala. *Expedition* 7(3):14-23.
1969 A new population estimate for Tikal, Guatemala. *Am. Antiq.* 34(4):429-433.
1972 Family size, prehistoric population estimates, and the ancient Maya. *Am. Antiq.* 37(1):135-139.

Hawley, Amos H.
1950 *Human Ecology: A Theory of Community Structure.* New York, The Ronald Press Company.

Henderson, John G.
1884 Aboriginal remains near Naples, Illinois. In *Annual Report of the Board of Regents of the Smithsonian Institution for the Year 1882,* pp. 686-721. Washington.

Hesselberth, Charles
1945 An Ohio type Hopewell ceremonial mound. *Ill. State Archaeol. Soc. J.,* n.s., 3(1):18-20.
1946 Notes on the Ogden-Fettie mounds. *Ill. State Archaeol. Soc. J.,* n.s., 4(1):9-11.

Hill, Frederick C.
1970 *An Analysis of Animal Remains From the Macoupin Site, Illinois.* M.S. thesis, Department of Biological Sciences, Illinois State University. Normal.

Houart, Gail L.
1971 An archaeological survey of the Apple, Mauvaise Terre and Big Sandy valleys, and selected parts of the lower Illinois River Valley. In *Preliminary Report of 1971 Historic Sites Survey Archaeological Reconnaissance of Selected Areas in the State of Illinois,* Part 1, Summary, pp. 54-61. Urbana, Ill., Illinois Archaeological Survey.

Howells, W. W.
1960 Estimating population numbers through archaeological and skeletal remains. In *The Application of Quantitative Methods in Archaeology,* Robert F. Heizer and Sherburne F. Cook (Eds.), pp. 158-185. Viking Fund Publications in Anthropology, No. 28. Chicago, Quadrangle Books.

Hunter, King B.
1965 Preliminary report on the Hopewellian skeletons from the Klunk site, Calhoun County, Illinois. *Proc. Indiana Acad. Sci.* 74:81-83.

Jamison, Paul Lytle
1971 A demographic and comparative analysis of the Albany mounds (Illinois) Hopewell skeletons. In *The Indian Mounds at Albany, Illinois,* Elaine Bluhm Herold (Ed.), pp. 107-153. Davenport Museum Anthropological Papers, No. 1. Davenport, Iowa.

Johnston, Francis E., and Charles E. Snow
1961 The reassessment of the age and sex of the Indian Knoll skeletal population: demographic and methodological aspects. *Am. J. Phys. Anthropol.* 19(3):237-244.

Keyfitz, Nathan
1968 *Introduction to the Mathematics of Population.* Reading, Mass., Addison-Wesley Publishing Company.

Kidder, Alfred Vincent
1958 *Pecos, New Mexico: Archaeological Notes.* Papers of the Robert S. Peabody Foundation for Archaeology, Vol. 5. Andover, Mass.

Kish, Leslie
1965 *Survey Sampling.* New York, John Wiley and Sons, Inc.

Klippel, Walter E.
1971 An archaeological survey of the lower-central Sangamon River drainage in central Illinois. In *Preliminary Report of 1971 Historic Sites Survey Archaeological Reconnaissance of Selected Areas in the State of Illinois*: Part 1, Summary, pp. 19-25. Urbana, Ill., Illinois Archaeological Survey.

Kroeber, Alfred L.
1939 *Cultural and Natural Areas of Native North America.* University of California Publications in American Archaeology and Ethnology, Vol. 38. Berkeley, University of California Press.

LeBlanc, Steven
1971 An addition to Naroll's suggested floor area and settlement population relationship. *Am. Antiq.* 36(2):210-211.

Lee, Richard B.
1968 What hunters do for a living, or how to make out on scarce resources. In *Man the Hunter,* Richard B. Lee and Irven DeVore (Eds.), pp. 30-48. Chicago, Aldine Publishing Company.

Lotka, Alfred J.
1939 *Theorie Analytique des Associations Biologiques, Pt. II: Analyse Démographique avec Application Particulière à l'Espèce Humaine.* Actualités Scientifiques et Industrielles, No. 780. Paris, Hermann and Cie.

McAdams, William, Jr.
1881 Ancient mounds of Illinois. *Proc. Am. Assoc. Adv. Sci.,* 29th Meeting (1880), pp. 710-718.
1884 Mounds of the Mississippi Bottom, Illinois. In *Annual Report of the Board of Regents of the Smithsonian Institution for the Year 1882,* pp. 684-686. Washington.

McArthur, Norma
1970 The demography of primitive populations. *Science* 167(3921):1097-1101.

McCarthy, Frederick D., and Margaret McArthur
1960 The food quest and the time factor in Aboriginal economic life. In *Records of the American-Australian Scientific Expedition to Arnhem Land,* Vol. 2, *Anthropology and Nutrition,* Charles P. Mountford (Ed.), pp. 145-194. Melbourne, Melbourne University Press.

McDonald, Charles
1944 Burials found in immense cave along Illinois

River in Calhoun County, Illinois. *Ill. State Archaeol. J.*, April:29-30.

McGregor, John C.
1958 *The Pool and Irving Villages: A Study of Hopewell Occupation in the Illinois River Valley.* Urbana, Ill., University of Illinois Press.

McKern, W. C., Paul F. Titterington,
and James B. Griffin
1945 Painted pottery figurines from Illinois. *Am. Antiq.* 10(3):295-302.

Middleton, James D.
1888 *Report of Mound Exploration in 1888– Illinois.* Manuscript on file at the Smithsonian Institution, National Anthropological Archives, Washington.

Mitchell, Brainerd
1880 Mounds of Pike County, Illinois. In *Annual Report of the Board of Regents of the Smithsonian Institution for the Year 1879*, pp. 367-368. Washington.

Mohrman, Harold W., and Leonard W. Blake
n.d. *Two Figurines From Jersey County, Illinois.* Manuscript on file at the Department of Anthropology, Northwestern University. Evanston, Ill.

Montet-White, Anta
1968 *The Lithic Industries of the Illinois Valley in the Early and Middle Woodland Period.* Anthropological Papers, No. 35. Ann Arbor, University of Michigan, Museum of Antrhopology.

Munson, Patrick J.
1971 An archaeological survey of the Wood River terrace and adjacent bottoms and bluffs in Madison County, Illinois. In *Archaeological Surveys of the American Bottoms and Adjacent Bluffs, Illinois*, pp. 1-17. Illinois State Museum Reports of Investigations, No. 21. Springfield.

Munson, Patrick J., Paul W. Parmalee,
and Richard A. Yarnell
1971 Subsistence ecology of Scovill, a terminal Middle Woodland village. *Am. Antiq.* 36(4):410-431.

Nag, Moni
1962 *Factors Affecting Human Fertility in Non-industrial Societies: A Cross-Cultural Study.* Yale University Publications in Anthropology, No. 66. New Haven.

Naroll, Raoul
1956 A preliminary index of social development. *Am. Anthropol.* 58(4):687-715.
1962 Floor area and settlement population. *Am. Antiq.* 27(4):587-589.

Ogden, J. Gordon, III, and Ruth J. Hay
1967 Ohio Wesleyan University natural radiocarbon measurements III. *Radiocarbon* 9:316-332.

Parmalee, Paul W., Andreas A. Paloumpis,
and Nancy Wilson
1972 *Animals Utilized by Woodland Peoples Occupying the Apple Creek Site, Illinois.* Illinois State Museum Reports of Investigations, No. 23, and Illinois Valley Archaeological Program Research Papers, Vol. 5. Springfield.

Perino, Gregory H.
1952 Field trip report. In *The Snyders Site, Calhoun County, Illinois*, pp. 9-10. St. Louis, The Greater St. Louis Archaeological Society.
1961 Tentative classification of plummets in the lower Illinois River Valley. *Central States Archaeol. J.* 8(2):43-56.
1962 A review of Calhoun County, Illinois, prehistory. *Wisconsin Archeol.* 43(2):44-51.
1964 The Peisker site, Calhoun County, Illinois. *Oklahoma Anthropol. Soc. Newsletter* 12(2):6-9.
1966a A preliminary report on the Peisker site, part 1–the Early Woodland occupation. *Central States Archaeol. J.* 13(2):47-51.
1966b A preliminary report on the Peisker site, part 2–the Hopewell occupation. *Central States Archaeol. J.* 13(3):84-89.
1966c A preliminary report on the Peisker site, part 3–The Historic Burials. *Central States Archaeol. J.* 13(4):126-129.
1968 The Pete Klunk mound group, Calhoun County, Illinois: the Archaic and Hopewell occupations. In *Hopewell and Woodland Site Archaeology in Illinois*, pp. 9-124. Illinois Archaeological Survey Bulletin, No. 6. Urbana, Ill.
1973a The Late Woodland component at the Pete Klunk site, Calhoun County, Illinois. In *Late Woodland Site Archaeology in Illinois I: Investigations in South-Central Illinois*, pp. 58-89. Illinois Archaeological Survey Bulletin, No. 9. Urbana, Ill.
1973b Gibson Mound 7, Calhoun County, Illinois. In *Late Woodland Site Archaeology in Illinois I: Investigations in South-Central Illinois*, pp. 211-213. Illinois Archaeological Survey Bulletin, No. 9. Urbana, Ill.
n.d.[a] *Hopewellian Sites in Western Illinois.* Manuscript on file at the Department of Anthropology, Northwestern University. Evanston, Ill.
n.d.[b] *Meppen Mound Group, Calhoun County, Ill.* Manuscript on file at the Department of Anthropology, Northwestern University. Evanston, Ill.

Powell, B. Bruce
1957 Hopewellian pottery of the lower Illinois Valley: the Snyders site ceramics. *Pap. Michigan Acad. Sci. Arts Lett.* 42:219-224.

Rackerby, Frank
1969 *Preliminary Report on the Macoupin Site: A Lower Illinois Valley Middle Woodland Settlement.* Paper presented at the Society for American Archaeology meetings, May 1-3, 1969, Milwaukee.

Ricketson, Oliver G., Jr.
1937 The Excavations in Uaxactun, Guatemala, Group E–1926-1931. *Carnegie Inst. Washington Publ.* 477(Part 1):1-180.

Rinaldo, John Beach
1937 *The Pere Marquette Park Site.* M.A. thesis, Department of Anthropology, University of Chicago. Chicago.

Rubey, William W.
  1952 *Geology and Mineral Resources of the Hardin and Brussels Quadrangles (in Illinois).* Geological Survey Professional Paper, No. 218. Washington, U.S. Department of Interior.

Sahlins, Marshall D.
  1958 *Social Stratification in Polynesia.* American Ethnological Society Monographs, No. 29. Seattle, University of Washington Press.
  1972 *Stone Age Economics.* Chicago, Aldine-Atherton, Inc.

Sanders, William T., and Joseph Marino
  1970 *New World Prehistory: Archaeology of the American Indian.* Englewood Cliffs, N.J., Prentice-Hall, Inc.

Sanders, William T., and Barbara J. Price
  1968 *Mesoamerica: The Evolution of a Civilization.* New York, Random House.

Service, Elman R.
  1962 *Primitive Social Organization.* New York, Random House.

Shalkop, Robert L.
  1949 *The Jersey Bluff Archaeological Focus, Jersey County, Illinois.* M.A. research paper, Department of Anthropology, University of Chicago. Chicago.

Shetrone, Henry Clyde
  1930 *The Mound-Builders.* New York, D. Appleton and Company.

Smith, Philip E. L.
  1972 Changes in population pressure in archaeological explanation. *World Archaeol.* 4(1):5-18.

Snow, Charles E.
  1948 Indian Knoll skeletons of Site Oh 2, Ohio County, Kentucky. *Univ. Kentucky Rep. Anthropol.* 4(3):367-555.

Snyder, John Francis
  1883 Indian Remains in Cass County, Illinois. In *Annual Report of the Board of Regents of the Smithsonian Institution for the Year 1881,* pp. 568-579. Washington.
  1894 Buried deposits of hornstone disks. *Proc. Am. Assoc. Adv. Sci.,* 42nd meeting (1893), pp. 318-324.
  1895a A group of Illinois mounds. *The Archaeologist* 3(3):77-81.
  1895b A group of Illinois mounds. *The Archaeologist* 3(4):109-113.
  1898 A group of Illinois mounds. *Am. Archaeol.* 2(1):16-23.

Stevenson, Robert F.
  1968 *Population and Political Systems in Tropical Africa.* New York, Columbia University Press.

Steward, Julian H.
  1955 *Theory of Culture Change.* Urbana, University of Illinois Press.

Struever, Stuart
  1960 *The Kamp Mound Group and a Hopewell Mortuary Complex in the Lower Illinois Valley.* M.A. thesis, Department of Anthropology, Northwestern University. Evanston.
  1961 Further excavations at the Snyders site: an analysis of Snyders ceramics. *Central States Archaeol. J.* 8(3):94-100.

  1964 The Hopewell interaction sphere in Riverine-Western Great Lakes culture history. In *Hopewellian Studies,* Joseph R. Caldwell and Robert L. Hall (Eds.), pp. 85-106. Illinois State Museum Scientific Papers, Vol. 12, No. 3. Springfield.
  1965 Middle Woodland culture history in the Great Lakes Riverine area. *Am. Antiq.* 31(2): 211-223.
  1968a Problems, methods and organization: a disparity in the growth of archeology. In *Anthropological Archeology in the Americas,* Betty J. Meggers (ed.), pp. 131-151. Washington, Anthropological Society of Washington.
  1968b *A Re-examination of Hopewell in Eastern North America.* Ph.D. dissertation, Department of Anthropology, University of Chicago. Chicago.
  1968c Woodland subsistence-settlement systems in the lower Illinois Valley. In *New Perspectives in Archeology,* Sally R. Binford and Lewis R. Binford (Eds.), pp. 285-312. Chicago, Aldine Publishing Company.
  1970 Pioneer archaeology in an Illinois Middle Woodland mound. *Wisconsin Archeol.* 51(2):49-56.
  1971 Comments on archaeological data requirements and research strategy. *Am. Antiq.* 36(1):9-19.

Struever, Stuart, and Gail L. Houart
  1972 An analysis of the Hopewell interaction sphere. In *Social Exchange and Interaction,* Edwin N. Wilmsen (Ed.), pp. 47-79. Anthropological Papers, No. 46. Ann Arbor, Museum of Anthropology, University of Michigan.

Struever, Stuart, and Gregory H. Perino
  1968 The Meredosia obsidian core. *Michigan Archaeol.* 14(3-4):131-134.

Temple, Wayne C.
  1966 *Indian Villages of the Illinois Country.* Illinois State Museum Scientific Papers, Vol. 2, Part 2. Springfield.

Thomas, Cyrus
  1889 A mound in Calhoun County, Ill. *Science* 13(326):349.
  1894 Report on the mound explorations of the Bureau of Ethnology. In *Twelfth Annual Report of the Bureau of Ethnology to the Secretary of the Smithsonian Institution, 1890-1891,* by J. W. Powell, pp. 3-372. Washington.

Thompson, J. Eric S.
  1971 Estimates of Maya population: deranging factors. *Am. Antiq.* 36(2):214-216.

Thompson, Joe G.
  1968 Gallinipper cache blades. *Central States Archaeol. J.* 15(1):28-29.

Titterington, Paul F.
  1935 Certain bluff mounds of western Jersey County, Illinois. *Am. Antiq.* 1(1):6-46.
  1947 A tube pipe filter. *Ill. State Archaeol. Soc. J.* n.s., 4(3):20-21.
  n.d.[a] *The Andrew Snyders Mound Group and Village Site—Calhoun County, Illinois.* Notebook

on file at the Museum of Anthropology, University of Michigan. Ann Arbor.

n.d.[b] Notebooks on the Knight site excavations (4 vols.) on file at the Museum of Anthropology, University of Michigan. Ann Arbor.

n.d.[c] *Certain Bluff Mounds of Western Jersey County, Illinois.* Notebooks on file at the Illinois State Museum. Springfield.

United Nations

1954 *Demographic Yearbook,* sixth ed. New York.

1955 *Age and Sex Patterns of Mortality. Model Life-Tables for Under-Developed Countries.* Population Studies, No. 22 (ST/SOA/Series A/22). New York, U.N. Department of Economic and Social Affairs.

1956 *The Aging of Populations and Its Economic and Social Implications.* Population Studies, No. 26 (ST/SOA/Series A/26). New York, U.N. Department of Economic and Social Affairs.

1968 *The Concept of a Stable Population. Application to the Study of Populations of Countries with Incomplete Demographic Statistics.* Population Studies. No. 39 (ST/SOA/Series A/39). New York, U.N. Department of Economic and Social Affairs.

Vallois, Henri V.

1960 Vital statistics in prehistoric populations as determined from archaeological data. In *The Application of Quantitative Methods in Archaeology,* Robert F. Heizer and Sherburne F. Cook (Eds.), pp. 186-222. Viking Fund Publications in Anthropology, No. 28. Chicago, Quadrangle Books.

Wadlow, Walter L., and Gray LaDassor

1951 Excavation Merigan mound, Calhoun County, Illinois. *Greater St. Louis Archaeol. Soc. Bull.* 6:19-23.

Weiss, Kenneth M.

1973 *Demographic Models for Anthropology.* Memoirs of the Society for American Archaeology, No. 27. Washington.

Wilkinson, Richard Guy

1971 *Prehistoric Biological Relationships in the Great Lakes Region.* Anthropological Papers, No. 43. Ann Arbor, Museum of Anthropology, University of Michigan.

Wittry, Warren L.

1964 Northern Mississippi Valley. *In* Current Research, Charles E. Borden (Ed.). *Am. Antiq.* 29(4):543-547.

Woodburn, James

1968 An introduction to Hadza ecology. In *Man the Hunter,* Richard B. Lee and Irven DeVore (Eds.), pp. 49-55. Chicago, Aldine Publishing Company.

Wray, Donald E., and Richard S. MacNeish

1961 *The Hopewellian and Weaver occupations of the Weaver Site, Fulton County, Illinois,* Warren L. Wittry (Ed.). Illinois State Museum Scientific Papers, Vol. 7, No. 2, Springfield.

Wrigley, E. A.

1969 *Population and History.* New York, McGraw-Hill Book Company.

Yengoyan, Aram A.

1968 Demographic and ecological influences on aboriginal Australian marriage sections. In *Man the Hunter,* Richard B. Lee and Irven DeVore (Eds.), pp. 185-199. Chicago, Aldine Publishing Company.

Zawacki, April Allison, and Glenn Hausfater

1969 *Early Vegetation of the Lower Illinois Valley.* Illinois State Museum Reports of Investigations, No. 17, and Illinois Valley Archaeological Program Research Papers, Vol. 1. Springfield.

Zelinsky, Wilbur

1966 *A Prologue to Population Geography.* Englewood Cliffs, N.J., Prentice-Hall, Inc.

Zubrow, Ezra B. W.

1971 Carrying capacity and dynamic equilibrium in the prehistoric Southwest. *Am. Antiq.* 36(2):127-138.